APPLE AIRPODS PRO 2 USER GUIDE

The Intersection of Style and Functionality
in Modern Wearables

KATE T. RANDY

COPYRIGHT

TABLE OF CONTENTS

INTRODUCTION

Apple AirPods Pro 2 – A Game-Changer in Personal Audio

When Apple first introduced the AirPods back in 2016, the world of personal audio underwent a massive shift. They revolutionized the way we think about wireless audio devices. The sleek, minimalist design, the ease of use, and the seamless integration with Apple's ecosystem made them a runaway success. But with every new release, Apple has not only maintained the momentum but elevated it. The AirPods Pro 2, introduced in late 2022, are the next evolution in the AirPods lineup, taking everything that made the original AirPods Pro so beloved and pushing the boundaries even further.

In this book, we'll delve into the remarkable features, advanced technologies, and the future of Apple's AirPods Pro 2, examining what makes them not just another pair of wireless earbuds, but a game-changer for both casual listeners and audiophiles alike. Whether you're a long-time Apple fan or a newcomer to the AirPods family, this guide will walk you through everything you need to know, from the design and sound quality to the hidden gems of accessibility features.

A Revolution in Sound and Comfort

The AirPods Pro 2 build upon the legacy of their predecessors, offering a combination of comfort, sound quality, and cutting-edge technology that is hard to beat. With their improved Active Noise Cancellation (ANC), better sound, and integration of personalized audio experiences, the AirPods Pro 2 have raised the bar for what users can expect from in-ear headphones.

But it's not just about the audio. These earbuds are designed with your entire listening experience in mind. The AirPods Pro 2 include multiple sizes of silicone tips to ensure a snug fit and excellent sound isolation, so you can enjoy your favorite music, podcasts, or calls without distraction. The added benefits of Adaptive Transparency and the new Adaptive Audio feature allow users to have a customized experience tailored to their surroundings. It's not just an evolution in sound quality – it's an evolution in how we engage with our environment through music.

Designed for All: Comfort, Fit, and Accessibility

One of the standout features of the AirPods Pro 2 is their design. With a streamlined case that is slightly smaller than the original, and a refined in-ear design with a choice of sizes for a perfect fit, these earbuds cater to all types of users.

Whether you're someone who listens to music during a workout, someone who uses their earbuds to attend virtual meetings, or someone who just wants high-quality sound while commuting, the AirPods Pro 2 deliver a personalized experience.

The AirPods Pro 2 aren't just about how they look or sound, however. Apple has embedded accessibility features directly into these earbuds, making them an inclusive product for all users. Features such as Conversation Awareness and the clinical-grade hearing test – which allows users to check for mild to moderate hearing loss – are built right in, reflecting Apple's commitment to making their products accessible to a broader audience. The integration of these features demonstrates the brand's increasing emphasis on health and well-being, something that has been a cornerstone of the company's evolving approach to technology.

In fact, the AirPods Pro 2 serve as more than just a tool for listening. They have become an integral part of users' health routines, whether it's through the new hearing health functionalities or simply helping individuals focus in loud environments through ANC. The idea that something as small as a pair of earbuds can enhance the quality of life for so many is a testament to Apple's forward-thinking design philosophy.

Advanced Technology at Your Fingertips

When it comes to technology, the AirPods Pro 2 are at the cutting edge. Powered by the new H2 chip, these earbuds offer better sound, improved noise cancellation, and quicker response times. The H2 chip allows for faster pairing, greater efficiency, and higher audio quality, making it a crucial upgrade from the previous generation. The chip also plays a key role in the AirPods Pro 2's ability to adapt to different environments, adjusting the noise-canceling and transparency modes based on the sounds around you.

The integration of Personalized Spatial Audio with dynamic head tracking is another hallmark feature of the AirPods Pro 2. This technology creates an immersive listening experience that feels like you're right in the middle of the music, with sound moving naturally around you as you turn your head. Whether you're watching a movie, playing a game, or listening to your favorite album, Personalized Spatial Audio takes your experience to the next level, offering a richer and more dynamic soundstage.

Noise Cancellation Like Never Before

Active Noise Cancellation has been a staple of the AirPods Pro from the very beginning, but Apple has truly outdone itself with the AirPods Pro 2. Thanks to the H2 chip, the second-generation AirPods Pro now offer up to twice as much noise cancellation as their predecessors. This means that whether you're sitting on a crowded subway or working in a busy coffee shop, you'll be able to enjoy your audio without interference from the outside world. The ability to block out external noise is critical for people who rely on their earbuds for concentration, whether for work or leisure, and the AirPods Pro 2 ensure that you can achieve a high level of focus, even in chaotic environments.

But Apple didn't stop there. The addition of Adaptive Transparency allows the AirPods Pro 2 to automatically adjust how much external sound you hear. If you're walking on a busy street and need to stay aware of your surroundings, Adaptive Transparency lets in just enough ambient noise for you to stay safe without interrupting your music or podcast. This makes the AirPods Pro 2 incredibly versatile, striking the perfect balance between immersion and awareness.

A Glimpse Into the Future of Wireless Earbuds

The release of the AirPods Pro 2 represents just one step in Apple's larger vision for the future of wireless audio. With each new iteration of AirPods, Apple continues to refine and enhance the listening experience, pushing the boundaries of what's possible with wireless earbuds. Whether it's by improving sound quality, increasing battery life, or integrating more advanced health features, the AirPods Pro 2 serve as a prime example of the future direction of personal audio technology.

As we look ahead, it's clear that the next generation of wireless audio will be built around seamless integration, adaptability, and user customization. The AirPods Pro 2 already offer a glimpse into this future with their ability to adjust to various listening environments, provide spatially aware sound, and track health metrics all within the same device. The AirPods Pro 2 have set a new standard for personal audio, one that is only going to get better as technology continues to advance.

Why You Should Care About the AirPods Pro 2

For some, the AirPods Pro 2 are just another pair of wireless earbuds. But for many, these tiny devices represent a revolution in personal audio, health, and connectivity. The AirPods Pro 2 are not only about delivering excellent sound quality – they are about enhancing your life in ways that you might not have considered before. They are about being able to block out distractions while you work, hearing your music in a way that feels natural and immersive, and even taking control of your hearing health in an easy-to-use and unobtrusive way.

Whether you're a student looking for a tool to help you focus, a professional who needs high-quality audio for calls and meetings, or a music lover who wants the best possible listening experience, the AirPods Pro 2 have something to offer. These earbuds are more than just a gadget – they are a reflection of how far technology has come and a preview of the exciting possibilities that lie ahead in the world of personal audio.

In the chapters ahead, we will take a deeper dive into the technical aspects, features, and real-world applications of the AirPods Pro 2. From the H2 chip to the new Adaptive Audio features, we'll break down the advanced technologies that make these earbuds stand out. Along the way, we'll share user experiences, expert opinions, and tips for getting the most out of your AirPods Pro 2. By the end of this book, you'll have a full understanding of how these earbuds work, why they matter, and how they can improve your daily life. Welcome to the world of Apple AirPods Pro 2 – let's dive in!

CHAPTER 1

The Genesis of AirPods

Apple's influence on the tech world is undeniable, and the introduction of the AirPods is one of the most significant moments in the history of personal audio. With the AirPods, Apple didn't just create a new product; they created an entirely new category of personal technology. A revolution in how we experience audio, and an evolution of the wireless earbuds concept, Apple's AirPods became a pop culture phenomenon, making it clear that the company's approach to consumer electronics was both cutting-edge and transformative.

This chapter will explore the birth of the AirPods, their evolution from the original model to the AirPods Pro, and the exciting innovations brought forth with the announcement of the AirPods Pro 2. We will take you on a journey that spans from the initial disruption in wireless audio to the development of the AirPods Pro 2, a product that embodies the future of wireless earbuds.

1.1 The Birth of a Revolution: How Apple Transformed Wireless Audio

In 2016, Apple made an audacious move that many thought was risky: they removed the 3.5mm headphone jack from their flagship product, the iPhone 7. While this move received its share of criticism and concern from the public, it set the stage for the wireless audio revolution. Apple, never one to back down from a challenge, wasn't simply removing a feature from their device – they were laying the groundwork for the future of wireless technology.

The Era of Wireless Audio Begins

Before the iPhone 7, wireless audio was an afterthought. Bluetooth headphones existed, but they were clunky, uncomfortable, and plagued by poor sound quality and frequent connectivity issues. Apple, however, knew that the future of mobile technology was wireless, and they envisioned a future where users could listen to music, take calls, and interact with their devices without being tethered by wires.

The AirPods were launched in December 2016, and they were designed to complement the new iPhone 7, which had lost the headphone jack. The AirPods weren't the first Bluetooth earphones to hit the market, but they were the first to offer the seamless integration and user experience that Apple is known for. These earbuds were designed to work perfectly with the iPhone and other Apple devices, providing a wireless audio experience that was easy, reliable, and convenient.

The AirPods' most notable feature was their instant pairing. When you opened the AirPods case near your iPhone, a simple prompt appeared on your screen, asking if you wanted to connect. There was no need to fiddle with Bluetooth settings or worry about compatibility issues – everything was done for you in a single, fluid motion. This user-friendly experience became a cornerstone of the AirPods' success and set the stage for all subsequent wireless earbuds that would follow.

In addition to ease of use, the AirPods offered impressive sound quality for their size. They featured custom-designed drivers and a dual beamforming microphone system to deliver rich sound and crisp voice clarity. Despite their small size, the AirPods quickly became known for their sound performance, which was enhanced by Apple's focus on creating a compact and portable product without sacrificing audio quality.

Breaking Into Pop Culture

Apple's marketing machine worked its magic, and the AirPods quickly became more than just a product – they became a cultural symbol. They were seen as the must-have accessory for iPhone users, and their white, minimalist design soon became synonymous with the Apple brand. People began to wear them everywhere, from the gym to the streets, and even in movies and television shows.

The AirPods' popularity exploded, and soon after their release, they became ubiquitous. They weren't just a functional piece of technology – they were a lifestyle accessory. AirPods became a status symbol, often seen as a representation of modernity and innovation. Their distinct look, combined with Apple's loyal customer base and consistent product quality, cemented the AirPods' place as the wireless audio standard.

1.2 From Concept to Icon: The Evolution from AirPods to AirPods Pro

While the original AirPods were a success, Apple wasn't content to rest on its laurels. In 2019, just three years after the initial launch, Apple introduced a new version of the AirPods – the AirPods Pro. This wasn't just a minor update; it was a major redesign that took the AirPods from a simple, convenient wireless earbud to a full-fledged audio product that offered premium features for audiophiles and casual listeners alike.

The AirPods Pro – The Next Step in Audio Evolution

The AirPods Pro were released in October 2019, and they introduced several key features that weren't available in the original AirPods. The most significant change was the inclusion of Active Noise Cancellation (ANC), a technology that blocks out ambient noise to create a more immersive listening experience. This was a game-changer for the AirPods, making them a serious competitor in the premium earbud market, where noise-canceling technology had previously been limited to over-ear headphones.

The AirPods Pro also introduced a new, more ergonomic design with three sizes of silicone ear tips, ensuring a better fit for a wider range of ear shapes. This was a huge improvement over the one-size-fits-all design of the original AirPods, which, while comfortable for many, didn't provide a secure fit for all users. The silicone tips on the AirPods Pro helped create a better seal in the ear, improving sound quality and noise isolation.

In addition to ANC, the AirPods Pro included a Transparency mode that allowed users to hear the outside world when necessary. This was particularly useful in situations where you might want to be aware of your surroundings, such as when walking on busy streets or during conversations. Transparency mode worked by using external microphones to let ambient sounds filter through, ensuring that users could still engage with the world around them while enjoying their music.

Sound quality was another area where the AirPods Pro excelled. They featured a custom high-excursion driver and a high-performance amplifier, delivering deep bass, crisp highs, and balanced mids. The sound quality was noticeably superior to the original AirPods, and the inclusion of Adaptive EQ, which automatically adjusts the sound based on the fit of the ear tips, made them even more impressive.

The AirPods Pro were also equipped with the Apple H1 chip, which enabled faster connectivity, improved battery life, and support for features like "Hey Siri" hands-free functionality. The H1 chip also allowed for automatic switching between Apple devices, ensuring that users could easily transition between their iPhone, iPad, and Mac without having to manually reconnect their earbuds.

Apple's Continued Push for Innovation

While the AirPods Pro represented a major leap forward, Apple wasn't done yet. With every iteration of the AirPods, the company pushed the boundaries of what wireless earbuds could do. The AirPods Pro were a clear indication that Apple was committed to making premium wireless earbuds accessible to a wider audience, combining luxury with functionality in a way that few other companies had done before.

As the AirPods Pro gained traction in the market, it was clear that Apple was carving out a new niche in the audio world – one where performance, convenience, and design could coexist. The AirPods Pro weren't just another pair of earbuds; they were a product that bridged the gap between casual consumers and audiophiles, offering advanced features without sacrificing simplicity or ease of use.

1.3 The AirPods Pro 2 Announcement: A New Era Begins

In September 2022, Apple unveiled the highly anticipated successor to the AirPods Pro – the AirPods Pro 2. While the first-generation AirPods Pro had already set a high bar, Apple's second-generation model raised the stakes even further with new features, improved sound quality, and enhancements that addressed some of the most common user requests.

The AirPods Pro 2 – A Leap Into the Future

The AirPods Pro 2 retained the same familiar design and form factor of the original model but introduced several key upgrades. The most significant of these was the new H2 chip, which replaced the H1 chip found in the original AirPods Pro. The H2 chip enabled even better sound quality, improved noise cancellation, and more efficient power management, all while maintaining the seamless integration with Apple devices that users had come to love.

Enhanced Active Noise Cancellation and Transparency Mode

One of the standout features of the AirPods Pro 2 is the improvement in Active Noise Cancellation (ANC). Apple claimed that the AirPods Pro 2 could block out twice as much ambient noise as the first-generation model, creating an even more immersive listening experience. This enhancement was especially noticeable in noisy environments, such as airports or crowded public spaces, where the ANC helped users fully engage with their music or podcasts.

The Transparency mode was also upgraded in the AirPods Pro 2, offering a more natural sound experience when you need to be aware of your surroundings. Adaptive Transparency, which automatically adjusts the level of outside noise based on your environment, was introduced to provide a more customized experience. This was particularly useful for people who use their AirPods Pro 2 during activities like running or cycling, where situational awareness is crucial.

Personalized Sound and Improved Battery Life

In addition to ANC and Transparency, the AirPods Pro 2 featured Personalized Spatial Audio with dynamic head tracking. This feature allowed users to experience 3D audio that was customized to their ears, making movies, music, and games feel more immersive than ever before. Personalized Spatial Audio also included an option to perform a hearing test, allowing the AirPods Pro 2 to adjust the sound profile based on your unique hearing ability, ensuring the best possible audio experience.

Battery life was another area where the AirPods Pro 2 made significant strides. With up to six hours of listening time on a single charge, users could enjoy longer sessions without needing to recharge. The improved charging case, which now featured a USB-C port, also allowed for quicker charging, ensuring that users could get back to their music or calls faster than before.

A New Era of Wireless Audio

The announcement of the AirPods Pro 2 marked the beginning of a new era for wireless audio. Apple had once again raised the bar for what users could expect from wireless earbuds, incorporating cutting-edge features like personalized sound, improved ANC, and advanced integration with the Apple ecosystem. With the AirPods Pro 2, Apple reinforced its commitment to pushing the boundaries of what's possible in personal audio.

The release of the AirPods Pro 2 was met with excitement from both long-time Apple fans and new customers alike. They were not just an upgrade; they were a redefinition of what truly premium wireless earbuds could be.

In this chapter, we've traced the journey of Apple's AirPods from their birth as a revolution in wireless audio to the evolution of the AirPods Pro, and finally, the monumental release of the AirPods Pro 2. As we move forward, we'll explore the unique features and innovations that make the AirPods Pro 2 the gold standard in personal audio. Whether you're a new user or a seasoned AirPods fan, the next chapter will dive deeper into the unparalleled features of these groundbreaking earbuds.

CHAPTER 2

The Heartbeat – H2 Chip and Adaptive Audio

Apple's AirPods Pro 2 are not just an iteration of the previous model—they are a leap into the future of personal audio. At the heart of these advancements lies the new H2 chip, a crucial component that has enabled the AirPods Pro 2 to push boundaries in sound quality, noise cancellation, and personalization. In this chapter, we'll explore how the H2 chip works, its role in creating the exceptional sound experience of the AirPods Pro 2, and how Adaptive Audio and Personalized Spatial Audio take this experience to the next level.

2.1 Understanding the H2 Chip: The Power Behind the Sound

To fully appreciate the AirPods Pro 2, it's essential to understand the significance of the new H2 chip. Apple has long been known for designing its own chips for iPhones, iPads, and Macs, and the H2 chip is a natural extension of this philosophy. It's the driving force behind several of the AirPods Pro 2's innovations, powering everything from enhanced sound quality to more effective noise cancellation.

The Evolution of Apple's Chipsets

Apple's approach to chip development began with the A-series chips used in iPhones, but with the H-series chips, Apple took a more targeted approach, designing chips specifically for the AirPods. The original AirPods used the W1 chip, which made the pairing process simple and seamless with Apple devices. Then came the H1 chip in the first-generation AirPods Pro, which brought with it features like "Hey Siri" support and the ability to automatically switch between devices.

The H2 chip in the AirPods Pro 2 builds on these previous innovations and brings even greater capabilities. The H2 is optimized for audio processing and helps Apple achieve improvements across the board in the AirPods Pro 2. Whether it's sound quality, noise cancellation, or the new personalized listening features, the H2 chip makes all of this possible.

Enhanced Sound Quality

One of the most significant advancements provided by the H2 chip is an enhanced audio experience. The H2 chip enables better sound performance by improving the drivers, amplifiers, and overall signal processing of the AirPods Pro 2. Apple has designed the H2 chip to deliver richer bass, crisper highs, and clearer mids. This results in a more balanced and full sound profile that appeals to a wide range of music genres and audio content.

Thanks to the H2 chip's processing power, the AirPods Pro 2 can now perform real-time adjustments to sound quality, ensuring that the audio is always optimized for the content you're listening to. Whether you're enjoying music, watching a movie, or playing a game, the H2 chip adapts to deliver the best audio possible.

Improved Noise Cancellation

Noise cancellation in the AirPods Pro 2 has seen a significant upgrade, thanks in large part to the H2 chip. Active Noise Cancellation (ANC) is one of the defining features of the AirPods Pro series, and with the H2 chip, Apple has taken it to the next level. The H2 chip's faster processing capabilities allow for more effective cancellation of external noise, blocking out ambient sounds more efficiently than before.

The chip works in tandem with the custom-built drivers and microphones to create an immersive listening environment by detecting and canceling unwanted noise. This improvement in ANC means that users can experience the same high-quality sound they would get in a soundproof room, even when surrounded by distracting noises like traffic, chatter, or the hum of a plane.

Efficient Power Consumption

Another advantage of the H2 chip is its energy efficiency. The H2 is designed to manage power more effectively, which leads to better battery life. Despite the increased processing power and enhanced features, the AirPods Pro 2 can still deliver up to six hours of listening time on a single charge, a significant improvement over the original AirPods Pro. The chip's power optimization also helps maintain high performance while minimizing power consumption, ensuring you get the most out of your AirPods Pro 2 without constantly worrying about charging.

2.2 Adaptive Audio Explained: Seamless Listening in Every Environment

One of the standout features of the AirPods Pro 2 is Adaptive Audio, a feature that automatically adjusts the audio experience based on your surroundings. This feature builds on the idea of noise cancellation but goes a step further by making it more dynamic and responsive to the environment you're in. This ensures a seamless listening experience no matter where you are, whether you're walking through a busy city street, sitting in a quiet office, or relaxing at home.

What is Adaptive Audio?

Adaptive Audio is an intelligent audio system that combines elements of Active Noise Cancellation (ANC) and Transparency Mode, continuously adjusting to the noise level in your environment. In simple terms, it allows the AirPods Pro 2 to intelligently determine how much external noise you need to hear and how much should be blocked out based on your current activity or location. The result is an optimized listening experience that is both immersive and safe.

How Does Adaptive Audio Work?

The AirPods Pro 2 feature multiple microphones that constantly listen to your environment. These microphones pick up sounds from the surroundings and feed that data into the H2 chip. The chip processes this data in real time and adjusts the noise-canceling level accordingly. For instance, if you're in a noisy environment, the AirPods Pro 2 will increase ANC to block out more noise. On the other hand, if you're in a quieter area, the system will decrease ANC and allow more of the outside sounds to pass through via Transparency Mode.

What makes Adaptive Audio so special is that it adapts automatically. You don't have to manually switch between

ANC and Transparency Mode as you move between environments. The AirPods Pro 2 will determine the ideal settings for you, giving you the perfect balance between immersion and awareness without the need for constant adjustments. For example, when you're walking outside, Adaptive Audio may reduce the ANC to let you hear the sounds of traffic or conversations, ensuring your safety. However, if you're sitting in a noisy café, it will enhance the ANC, so you can focus on your audio content without any distractions.

Why Adaptive Audio Matters

In a world where our environments are constantly changing, the ability to tailor your listening experience to your surroundings is incredibly valuable. It means you don't have to manually adjust your earbuds or take them out to be aware of your surroundings. Adaptive Audio allows you to stay immersed in your audio content while remaining aware of critical external sounds, providing the ideal balance between isolation and situational awareness.

Moreover, Adaptive Audio provides convenience. No longer will you need to worry about switching between ANC and Transparency Mode when you're moving from one location to another. Whether you're commuting, working, or exercising, the AirPods Pro 2 will automatically adjust the settings, saving you the hassle of constant adjustments.

2.3 Personalized Spatial Audio: Tailoring Sound to Your Ears

Personalized Spatial Audio is perhaps one of the most exciting features introduced in the AirPods Pro 2. It takes the concept of surround sound and applies it in a way that's specifically tailored to the unique shape of your ears and head. This technology is designed to create an immersive 3D sound experience, making you feel like you're right in the middle of the action, whether you're listening to music, watching a movie, or gaming.

What is Personalized Spatial Audio?

Spatial audio has been around for a while, particularly in the home theater world, where it creates the effect of sound coming from different directions to create a surround-sound experience. However, with the advent of Apple's Personalized Spatial Audio, this technology is now available in a portable, in-ear form. Personalized Spatial Audio uses dynamic head tracking to adjust the audio so that the sound appears to come from different directions as you move your head.

The difference between regular spatial audio and Personalized Spatial Audio is that the latter tailors the sound specifically to the user's unique anatomy. By conducting a simple hearing test through the iPhone, the AirPods Pro 2 can create a customized sound profile based on the shape of your ears and the way you hear. This ensures that the sound you experience is as accurate and immersive as possible.

How Does Personalized Spatial Audio Work?

Personalized Spatial Audio uses dynamic head tracking to create an immersive 3D audio experience. The H2 chip in the AirPods Pro 2 works in real-time to adjust the sound as you move your head. This means that the sound you hear feels more natural, as though it is coming from the environment around you rather than directly from the earbuds. This effect is particularly noticeable when watching movies, as it allows sound to move with your head movements, creating a more lifelike experience.

To set up Personalized Spatial Audio, the AirPods Pro 2 use the Face ID technology of your iPhone to scan the shape of your ears. This scan helps to map out your personal audio profile. From there, the AirPods adjust the sound accordingly, making the experience as personalized as possible. For example, if you tend to hear higher frequencies less clearly, the AirPods will boost those frequencies to compensate, ensuring a more balanced listening experience.

Why Personalized Spatial Audio Matters

Personalized Spatial Audio elevates the listening experience, offering a level of immersion that was previously reserved for expensive, high-end sound systems. Whether you're enjoying a movie or listening to a song, the sound feels more natural and enveloping, as though you are part of the experience rather than just an observer.

The ability to personalize the spatial audio experience based on your unique hearing profile adds another layer of depth to the AirPods Pro 2. It makes the earbuds more than just a tool for listening to music – they become an extension of your hearing, allowing you to experience sound in a way that's tailored to you. For audiophiles and casual listeners alike, Personalized Spatial Audio offers a more enjoyable, immersive, and accurate listening experience.

A Revolution in Listening

With the H2 chip, Adaptive Audio, and Personalized Spatial Audio, the AirPods Pro 2 represent the future of wireless earbuds. These technologies combine to offer an unparalleled listening experience that adapts to your needs and surroundings while delivering high-quality, immersive sound that feels uniquely yours. Apple has once again set a new standard in personal audio, and the AirPods Pro 2 are leading the way.

As we move further into the world of personalized technology, the AirPods Pro 2 stand out as a shining example of how innovation can enhance our daily lives, making the listening experience more intelligent, immersive, and tailored to each user.

CHAPTER 3

Design and Comfort

When Apple first introduced the AirPods, it was clear that they were going to be more than just another pair of wireless earbuds. Their sleek, minimalist design quickly turned them into an accessory that was just as much about style as it was about functionality. However, with the release of the AirPods Pro 2, Apple has taken that design philosophy to new heights, refining the already-successful formula to create a product that is not only visually appealing but also more comfortable, durable, and user-friendly than ever before.

In this chapter, we'll explore the design and comfort of the AirPods Pro 2. From the subtle yet important design changes to the introduction of new ear tips and improvements in durability, this chapter will explain how Apple's attention to detail has enhanced the overall user experience of these wireless earbuds. Whether you're a first-time AirPods user or a long-time fan, the design of the AirPods Pro 2 is sure to impress, and we'll dive into the aspects that make it so special.

3.1 A Familiar Yet Refined Look: Subtle Changes That Matter

Apple's design philosophy has always focused on simplicity and elegance, and the AirPods Pro 2 are no exception. From the moment you hold them in your hands, it's clear that Apple has refined the design of their original AirPods Pro, making subtle changes that enhance the overall aesthetic and user experience.

The Case: Smaller and More Functional

One of the first things users will notice when they pick up the AirPods Pro 2 is the new charging case. The case has been made slightly smaller than the one that came with the first-generation AirPods Pro, making it more pocketable and easier to carry around. Apple has always prioritized portability, and this design change reflects that philosophy, allowing users to store their AirPods more easily without sacrificing the capacity of the charging case.

In addition to the smaller size, the case now features a few improvements that make it even more functional. The AirPods Pro 2 case now comes with a built-in speaker that emits a sound when activated through the "Find My" app. This addition makes it easier for users to locate the case if it gets misplaced. The case also includes a lanyard loop, making it possible to attach it to a bag or keychain for added convenience.

Another significant improvement to the case is the inclusion of a USB-C charging port. While the first-generation AirPods Pro relied on a Lightning port, the AirPods Pro 2 now use the more universal USB-C, which aligns with Apple's move toward standardizing charging ports across their product lineup. This change is particularly useful for users who own multiple devices that use USB-C charging cables, eliminating the need for different cables and simplifying the charging process.

The AirPods Pro 2: Subtle Tweaks to the Design

As for the AirPods Pro themselves, the design remains very similar to the original model. However, there are some small but notable adjustments that contribute to the overall comfort and aesthetics. The most noticeable change is the stem of the AirPods Pro 2, which has been shortened slightly compared to the original. This subtle adjustment creates a more streamlined look while still maintaining the signature style that has made AirPods so iconic.

Apple also enhanced the fit of the earbuds with a more ergonomic design, making them more comfortable to wear for extended periods. The AirPods Pro 2 continue to feature the signature white finish, which has become synonymous with Apple's product design, but now with a more polished and refined look. The slight redesign of the stem and the overall shape of the earbuds makes them feel more comfortable in the ear while also contributing to a more elegant, streamlined appearance.

3.2 The Importance of Fit: New Ear Tip Sizes for Every Ear

One of the most significant factors in determining the comfort and sound quality of wireless earbuds is how well they fit in your ears. In the case of the original AirPods Pro, Apple made a major step forward by including three sizes of silicone ear tips, allowing users to find a more customized fit compared to the one-size-fits-all design of many other wireless earbuds. However, with the AirPods Pro 2, Apple has taken this concept even further, offering even more flexibility in terms of fit and comfort.

Improved Silicone Ear Tips

The most significant improvement in terms of fit for the AirPods Pro 2 is the introduction of new, more varied silicone ear tip sizes. While the first-generation AirPods Pro offered small, medium, and large sizes, the AirPods Pro 2 now feature an additional extra-small size to accommodate a wider range of ear shapes. This change is crucial because one of the key factors in achieving optimal sound quality and noise cancellation is ensuring that the ear tips fit snugly and securely in the ear. By offering an extra-small option, Apple ensures that users with smaller ear canals can enjoy the same great sound and ANC performance as those with larger ears.

The Ear Tip Fit Test: Personalizing the Experience

Another useful feature that complements the new ear tip sizes is the ear tip fit test. The AirPods Pro 2 come with an updated version of the fit test, which uses the built-in microphones to detect whether the ear tips are providing a good seal. The fit test ensures that users get the best possible sound quality and noise isolation from their AirPods, as a poor seal can result in a compromised listening experience. This is especially important for features like Active Noise Cancellation (ANC), which relies on a secure fit to block out ambient noise effectively.

By performing the ear tip fit test, users can find the best ear tip size for their ears, ensuring a comfortable and secure fit. The updated test has been made more accurate with the inclusion of new sensors in the AirPods Pro 2, allowing for more precise measurements and a more personalized listening experience.

Comfort for Extended Use

Comfort is a key consideration when it comes to any pair of earbuds, especially when it comes to wearing them for extended periods of time. The AirPods Pro 2 have been designed with this in mind, offering a more ergonomic shape that allows them to fit more comfortably in the ear without causing discomfort. The addition of the extra-small ear tip option means that users with smaller ears no longer have to struggle with earbuds that are too large, making the AirPods Pro 2 a more inclusive product for a wider range of users.

The soft, flexible silicone ear tips also contribute to the overall comfort of the AirPods Pro 2. These ear tips not only provide a secure fit but also help to reduce pressure on the ear, making the earbuds more comfortable to wear during long listening sessions. Whether you're using the AirPods Pro 2 for a workout, a commute, or a long conference call, you'll appreciate how well they stay in place without causing any discomfort.

3.3 Durability and Usability: Built for Everyday Life

When it comes to wireless earbuds, durability is an essential consideration. After all, they are designed to be used on the go, whether you're commuting, working out, or traveling. Apple has made sure that the AirPods Pro 2 are built to withstand the rigors of everyday life while still delivering exceptional performance.

Water and Sweat Resistance

One of the key durability features of the AirPods Pro 2 is their improved water and sweat resistance. While the original AirPods Pro were rated with an IPX4 water resistance rating (meaning they could withstand splashes of water from any direction), the AirPods Pro 2 take it a step further with an IPX4 rating as well, ensuring that they can handle sweat during workouts or rain while still maintaining their performance. This makes them an excellent choice for active individuals who need earbuds that can handle physical activity.

The water resistance rating also ensures that the AirPods Pro 2 are suitable for a variety of environments, from the gym to the beach. Whether you're exercising outdoors or enjoying a jog in the rain, the AirPods Pro 2 are designed to handle the elements without compromising their performance.

Built to Last: Durability for the Long Haul

In addition to their water resistance, the AirPods Pro 2 are built with durability in mind. The earbuds feature a robust construction that can withstand drops, bumps, and everyday wear and tear. The materials used in the AirPods Pro 2, including high-quality plastics and reinforced components, ensure that the earbuds can hold up to frequent use without deteriorating quickly.

The charging case, too, is built for durability. It's made from high-quality materials that are designed to withstand accidental drops or impacts, and its compact size makes it easy to carry without worrying about damage. The case's improved hinge design also ensures that it stays intact over time, even with frequent use.

Usability: Seamless Integration with Your Daily Routine

Beyond durability, the AirPods Pro 2 are designed to be incredibly easy to use. From the moment you open the case, the AirPods automatically pair with your iPhone or other Apple device, ensuring a hassle-free experience. The updated H2 chip further improves the AirPods Pro 2's integration with the Apple ecosystem, allowing for seamless switching between devices and enhanced voice commands with "Hey Siri."

The touch controls on the stem of the AirPods Pro 2 are also incredibly intuitive. You can adjust the volume, skip tracks, or take calls with just a simple swipe or tap, making it easy to control your music or calls without ever having to reach for your phone. Additionally, the ability to activate Transparency mode or ANC with a simple press on the stem means you can quickly adjust to your environment, ensuring that your AirPods are always ready to adapt to your needs.

Long-Lasting Battery Life

Another key aspect of usability is battery life, and the AirPods Pro 2 deliver on this front as well. With up to six hours of listening time on a single charge and a charging case that provides up to 30 hours of total battery life, the AirPods Pro 2 are designed to last through even the longest days. Whether you're traveling, working, or exercising, the AirPods Pro 2 will keep you connected and immersed in your audio content without constantly needing to be recharged.

A Perfect Balance of Design, Comfort, and Durability

The AirPods Pro 2 represent the culmination of Apple's commitment to creating products that are not only stylish and functional but also comfortable and durable. With subtle design improvements, an enhanced fit, and robust durability features, the AirPods Pro 2 are the perfect wireless earbuds for anyone who values both performance and comfort. Whether you're using them for work, exercise, or leisure, the

AirPods Pro 2 are designed to seamlessly integrate into your everyday life, offering a truly exceptional audio experience.

CHAPTER 4

Battery Life and Charging Innovations

The AirPods Pro 2 have emerged as one of the most revolutionary wireless earbuds on the market, offering an unparalleled combination of sound quality, comfort, and cutting-edge technology. While features like Adaptive Audio and Personalized Spatial Audio are at the forefront of the product's appeal, there are other equally crucial innovations that make the AirPods Pro 2 a standout. One of the most important of these innovations is the remarkable improvement in battery life and charging capabilities, two areas where Apple has focused much of its attention to enhance user experience.

In this chapter, we will explore the various aspects of the AirPods Pro 2's battery life and charging system, including the extended listening time, the new USB-C charging case, and Apple's commitment to sustainability in design. These advancements are key to understanding how the AirPods Pro 2 are not just about incredible sound but also about making the overall experience more convenient, efficient, and eco-friendly.

4.1 Extended Listening Time: Up to 6 Hours on a Single Charge

When it comes to wireless earbuds, one of the most significant considerations for users is battery life. As we integrate earbuds into nearly every aspect of our lives—whether we're commuting, working out, or enjoying entertainment—having earbuds that can keep up with us throughout the day is essential. The AirPods Pro 2 deliver on this front by offering substantial improvements in battery life compared to the previous generation.

How Long Can the AirPods Pro 2 Last on a Single Charge?

The AirPods Pro 2 provide up to six hours of listening time on a single charge, a significant improvement over the original AirPods Pro, which offered just over four hours of listening time. This increase in battery life means that users can enjoy extended listening sessions without having to worry about constantly recharging their earbuds. Whether you're traveling long distances, attending a full-day meeting, or listening to music while working out, the AirPods Pro 2's six-hour battery life ensures that your listening experience remains uninterrupted for an extended period.

The Role of the H2 Chip in Battery Life

The extended battery life in the AirPods Pro 2 is made possible in part by the new H2 chip, which enhances the efficiency of the earbuds' power management. The H2 chip is designed to handle high-performance tasks such as processing sound and active noise cancellation while using less power. This efficiency allows the AirPods Pro 2 to deliver the best sound quality and ANC performance without draining the battery quickly.

In addition to improved power management, the H2 chip also works in conjunction with other components to ensure the earbuds consume less energy overall. By reducing the power consumption required for tasks like real-time audio adjustments and noise cancellation, the H2 chip contributes to the AirPods Pro 2's ability to deliver longer listening times, ensuring that users can enjoy their audio experience without constantly worrying about recharging.

ANC and Battery Life

While the AirPods Pro 2's extended listening time is impressive, it's important to note that features like Active Noise Cancellation (ANC) can impact battery life. ANC requires significant power to analyze ambient noise and generate anti-noise signals, which can drain battery life more quickly. However, thanks to the efficiency of the H2 chip, the AirPods Pro 2 still manage to maintain six hours of listening time even when ANC is engaged.

For users who prefer to save battery life while still enjoying a quality listening experience, the AirPods Pro 2 offer Adaptive Audio and Transparency modes, which consume less power than ANC. This flexibility allows users to choose the level of noise cancellation or environmental awareness they want, depending on the activity or surroundings, all while ensuring that battery life remains optimized.

Real-World Benefits of Extended Battery Life

For many users, the ability to use the AirPods Pro 2 for up to six hours without charging is a game-changer. Commuters, students, fitness enthusiasts, and travelers all stand to benefit from the extended battery life, as it allows them to use the earbuds throughout the day without the need to plug them in for a recharge. This long battery life eliminates the need to carry a charging case or power bank for most of the day, adding a level of convenience and freedom that wasn't possible with previous models of AirPods or other wireless earbuds on the market.

In practical terms, the six-hour listening time translates to roughly three full-length movies, several podcast episodes, or multiple workout sessions. For people who rely on their earbuds throughout the day, the ability to listen for extended periods without interruption significantly enhances the overall experience.

4.2 The USB-C Charging Case: A Step Toward Universal Compatibility

Another major change in the AirPods Pro 2 is the new USB-C charging case. While the first-generation AirPods Pro relied on a Lightning port for charging, the AirPods Pro 2 now feature a USB-C port, which brings significant advantages for users in terms of charging flexibility and convenience.

Why the Shift to USB-C?

The decision to switch to a USB-C charging case is part of Apple's broader move toward standardizing charging across its product lineup. USB-C has become the industry standard for many electronic devices, including smartphones, tablets, laptops, and accessories. By adopting USB-C, Apple is providing a more universal charging solution for its customers, especially for those who own multiple devices that already use USB-C ports.

For example, many modern Apple products, such as the latest iPads and MacBooks, have switched to USB-C as their charging port. By aligning the AirPods Pro 2's charging case with this standard, Apple is eliminating the need for multiple cables and chargers. Users who already have USB-C cables for their iPhones, iPads, or Macs can now charge their AirPods Pro 2 with the same cable, making their device management simpler and more efficient.

Charging Speed and Convenience

The switch to USB-C also offers benefits in terms of charging speed. While the exact charging times for the AirPods Pro 2 with a USB-C port are similar to those of previous models, USB-C ports tend to offer faster data transfer and more efficient charging compared to Lightning ports. This means that users can enjoy quicker recharges, especially when using a high-speed charger.

For those in a hurry, the ability to charge the AirPods Pro 2 via USB-C is particularly useful. Even if you only have a short period to top up the battery, USB-C charging ensures that your earbuds will be ready to go again quickly, whether you're in a rush to leave the house or need a quick charge during your workout.

Environmental Benefits of USB-C

The adoption of USB-C in the AirPods Pro 2 also has environmental benefits. By consolidating charging standards across devices, Apple is reducing the need for different cables and adapters. This not only makes it easier for users to manage their devices but also helps to cut down on electronic waste. As more consumers transition to USB-C chargers, the need for multiple proprietary charging cables diminishes, which can have a positive impact on the environment in the long run.

Additionally, the more universal nature of USB-C means that users are less likely to need to purchase additional cables, reducing consumer spending and promoting more sustainable practices in the tech industry.

4.3 Eco-Friendly Considerations: Sustainability in Design

Apple has long been committed to making its products more sustainable, and the AirPods Pro 2 are no exception. The company has made significant strides toward reducing the environmental impact of its devices by focusing on energy efficiency, responsible sourcing of materials, and reducing waste. The AirPods Pro 2 are part of this effort, with several design and manufacturing changes that reflect Apple's ongoing commitment to sustainability.

Use of Recycled Materials

One of the key ways that Apple has improved the sustainability of the AirPods Pro 2 is by incorporating recycled materials into the design. The company has worked to increase the use of recycled plastics, metals, and other materials in its products to reduce reliance on new raw materials and lower the environmental impact of production. In the case of the AirPods Pro 2, a significant percentage of the plastic components are made from recycled materials, helping to reduce the overall carbon footprint of the product.

Apple has also worked to reduce the environmental impact of the packaging used for the AirPods Pro 2. The packaging is made from recycled fibers, and the use of plastic in packaging has been minimized. This initiative is part of Apple's larger goal to have a net-zero carbon footprint across its entire supply chain and product lifecycle by 2030.

Energy Efficiency and Low-Carbon Footprint

The AirPods Pro 2 are designed to be energy efficient, ensuring that they use as little power as possible while delivering high performance. From the optimized performance of the H2 chip to the efficient charging system, every aspect of the AirPods Pro 2 has been engineered to minimize energy consumption. This focus on energy efficiency contributes to the overall reduction of the product's carbon footprint, making the AirPods Pro 2 a more sustainable option compared to other wireless earbuds on the market.

Apple has also made it a priority to ensure that its manufacturing processes are more sustainable. The company has made significant investments in renewable energy and energy-efficient technologies across its supply chain, further reducing the carbon emissions associated with the production of the AirPods Pro 2.

Apple's Ongoing Commitment to the Environment

The AirPods Pro 2 are just one example of Apple's commitment to sustainability. The company has made bold strides in reducing its environmental impact across all of its products, from the iPhone to the MacBook to the AirPods. Apple's efforts to reduce emissions, improve recycling, and increase the use of recycled materials are setting a new standard for environmental responsibility in the tech industry.

As part of its broader environmental goals, Apple has committed to making all of its products, including the AirPods Pro 2, carbon-neutral by 2030. This means that the company is working toward eliminating all carbon emissions associated with its products, from manufacturing and transportation to usage and disposal. The AirPods Pro 2 represent a significant step toward this goal, with their eco-friendly design and use of sustainable materials.

A New Era of Battery Life, Charging, and Sustainability

The AirPods Pro 2 are a perfect example of how Apple continues to push the envelope in terms of innovation and sustainability. With extended listening time, a universal USB-C charging case, and a focus on eco-friendly design, the AirPods Pro 2 are a perfect blend of cutting-edge technology and environmental responsibility. These advancements not only make the AirPods Pro 2 a more convenient and efficient product for users but also reflect Apple's ongoing commitment to sustainability and the reduction of its environmental impact.

Whether it's the impressive six-hour battery life, the faster and more efficient charging case, or the eco-conscious materials used in the design, the AirPods Pro 2 represent a step forward in both performance and environmental responsibility. Apple's continued focus on making its products more energy-efficient and sustainable ensures that the AirPods Pro 2 will not only continue to deliver an outstanding user experience but also contribute to a more sustainable future for the tech industry.

CHAPTER 5

Health and Accessibility Features

The AirPods Pro 2 are not just a technological marvel for music lovers and audiophiles, they also represent a significant breakthrough in how wireless earbuds can assist with hearing health and accessibility. Apple has long been committed to making its products inclusive and accessible, and the AirPods Pro 2 are a testament to that commitment. With features designed to enhance hearing, protect your ears, and improve everyday interactions, the AirPods Pro 2 have redefined the potential of wearable audio devices.

In this chapter, we will explore how the AirPods Pro 2 function as hearing aids, the revolutionary self-assessment hearing test that comes with them, and the Conversation Awareness and Protection features that make these earbuds invaluable tools for users seeking a seamless blend of advanced technology and enhanced communication. These features elevate the AirPods Pro 2 beyond being just a consumer tech product—they are now an essential tool for individuals looking to improve their hearing health and everyday experiences.

5.1 AirPods Pro 2 as Hearing Aids: FDA-Approved Over-the-Counter Hearing Aids

For years, hearing aids were reserved for individuals with significant hearing loss, often requiring professional intervention and costly prescriptions. However, with the AirPods Pro 2, Apple has made a bold step in the realm of hearing health by offering a product that is FDA-approved as an over-the-counter hearing aid. This shift is a significant milestone in making hearing aids more accessible and affordable for a wider range of people.

What Makes AirPods Pro 2 FDA-Approved Hearing Aids?

The FDA's approval of the AirPods Pro 2 as over-the-counter hearing aids represents a major shift in the way we approach hearing technology. Traditionally, hearing aids were prescription-based devices that required a visit to an audiologist for fitting, adjustments, and regular maintenance. The AirPods Pro 2, however, have been designed to work as hearing aids that anyone can purchase and use without needing a prescription. This approval is part of the FDA's broader efforts to make hearing aids more affordable and accessible to people with mild to moderate hearing loss.

The AirPods Pro 2 incorporate advanced features that make them capable of enhancing hearing in various environments. One of the most significant features is their ability to amplify sound selectively, allowing users to hear more clearly in specific situations. This capability is essential for individuals with mild hearing loss who may struggle to hear high-frequency sounds, like the voices of people speaking in noisy environments.

How Does It Work?

The AirPods Pro 2 utilize the built-in microphones and the H2 chip to provide adaptive sound amplification, which enhances speech intelligibility. The device can detect environmental sounds and filter them accordingly to ensure that important sounds, such as voices, are amplified without distorting other background noises. The amplification is customized to suit the user's hearing profile, helping those with hearing loss to hear more clearly in a variety of situations, including conversations, watching TV, or listening to music.

The addition of Adaptive Transparency mode means that users can be aware of their surroundings, which is particularly important for safety in environments like busy streets or crowded rooms. The AirPods Pro 2 offer an all-in-one solution for hearing assistance—whether you need help understanding speech in a noisy environment or simply want to experience clear sound on your own terms, the AirPods Pro 2 are designed to enhance your hearing experience.

Breaking Down Barriers

What's more revolutionary about this feature is the simplicity and affordability it brings to hearing health. No longer do individuals with mild to moderate hearing loss need to go through complicated and often expensive processes to receive hearing aids. The AirPods Pro 2 provide a discreet, convenient, and cost-effective solution, which helps to eliminate the stigma often associated with wearing traditional hearing aids. The ability to purchase and use the AirPods Pro 2 without medical intervention removes barriers to entry and allows users to take control of their hearing health in a more autonomous way.

5.2 The Hearing Test: A 5-Minute Self-Assessment

In addition to functioning as FDA-approved hearing aids, the AirPods Pro 2 include a groundbreaking feature that allows users to assess their own hearing health—a five-minute self-assessment hearing test. This test is designed to help users determine their hearing profile and customize their listening experience based on their unique hearing needs. By offering an easy and quick way to check for hearing loss, the AirPods Pro 2 empower users to take charge of their hearing health, right from the comfort of their home.

Why a Hearing Test Matters

The hearing test built into the AirPods Pro 2 allows users to assess their hearing capabilities with a simple and non-invasive process. Often, individuals may not realize they have mild hearing loss until it begins to affect their quality of life. Common signs of hearing loss include difficulty hearing high-pitched sounds, trouble following conversations in noisy environments, or the need to turn up the volume on televisions or music players.

By offering a quick, in-home hearing test, the AirPods Pro 2 encourage users to be proactive about their hearing health. While the test is not a replacement for a professional hearing assessment, it provides valuable insights that can help users determine whether they should seek further evaluation or if they can benefit from using the AirPods Pro 2 as hearing aids.

How the Test Works

The hearing test process is straightforward and accessible. Once you've connected your AirPods Pro 2 to your iPhone, you can launch the Hearing Test in the Settings app. The test takes only five minutes and involves listening to a series of tones played through the AirPods Pro 2 at varying frequencies and volumes. As you listen, you'll be asked to respond to whether or not you hear the sound at each frequency. The AirPods Pro 2 use this information to generate a personalized hearing profile that adjusts the amplification of certain frequencies to match your specific hearing needs.

The hearing test also takes into account factors like ear shape and the fit of the ear tips. Since everyone's ears are different, the test ensures that your hearing profile is as accurate as possible by considering the ear's anatomy, ensuring that the sound adjustments are optimized for your unique hearing experience.

Customized Sound Based on Your Hearing

Once the hearing test is completed, the AirPods Pro 2 will automatically adjust their settings to better suit your hearing profile. The adjustments are subtle but effective—amplifying high frequencies that may be harder for you to hear while leaving other frequencies unaffected. These personalized adjustments ensure that you can enjoy audio content with clarity, without straining or overcompensating by turning up the volume. The result is an experience that feels more natural and tailored to your hearing, whether you're listening to music, podcasts, or engaging in conversations.

By offering this self-assessment hearing test, Apple is democratizing access to personalized hearing care. It allows users to get a clearer picture of their hearing health and make informed decisions about how to manage it. The convenience and accessibility of this feature ensure that hearing health is no longer something that only happens in a doctor's office—it's now something you can actively monitor and improve on your own terms.

5.3 Conversation Awareness and Protection: Enhancing Everyday Interactions

In addition to their hearing aid functionality, the AirPods Pro 2 come equipped with features designed to enhance your interactions with others and protect your hearing in everyday situations. These features, such as Conversation Awareness and Protection, not only improve the overall usability of the earbuds but also ensure that users are more connected to their environment and the people around them.

Conversation Awareness: Elevating Social Interactions

Conversation Awareness is one of the key accessibility features in the AirPods Pro 2, designed to help users engage in conversations more naturally without needing to remove their earbuds. This feature is especially valuable for people who wear earbuds regularly and often struggle to hear conversations while using them. With Conversation Awareness, the AirPods Pro 2 detect when you are speaking or when someone is trying to talk to you and automatically lower the volume of your music or podcast. This allows you to hear the other person clearly while still keeping your AirPods Pro 2 in place.

The way Conversation Awareness works is simple yet effective: the microphones in the AirPods Pro 2 pick up the sound of voices and understand when they're coming from a nearby person. The earbuds then adjust the audio levels accordingly, lowering the music or other audio content to make way for the conversation. This means you don't have to manually pause your audio or remove the AirPods Pro 2 to engage with others. The feature makes conversations easier and more natural, especially in social settings where you may be multitasking or need to listen to someone while still enjoying your audio.

Hearing Protection: Preserving Your Hearing Health

Hearing protection is an essential aspect of maintaining long-term ear health, and the AirPods Pro 2 incorporate features that help protect your hearing during extended listening sessions. While the AirPods Pro 2 are designed to deliver exceptional sound quality, Apple has taken steps to ensure that users don't put their hearing at risk by listening to audio at dangerously high volumes.

Volume Limiting and Sound Quality Management

One of the ways the AirPods Pro 2 protect hearing is through volume limiting features. While the earbuds allow users to enjoy high-quality sound, they also include safeguards that prevent users from turning up the volume to levels that could cause hearing damage over time. In addition, the AirPods Pro 2 feature sound quality management algorithms that adjust the audio output to maintain clarity without excessive volume. This ensures that users enjoy the full depth and richness of their audio without overloading their eardrums.

The AirPods Pro 2 also use Adaptive EQ technology to optimize the sound profile based on the fit and the sound environment. This means that users don't have to crank up the volume to hear subtle details in music or podcasts, thereby reducing the risk of hearing damage from prolonged high-volume listening.

Transparency Mode and Awareness

Transparency mode also plays an important role in protecting hearing. In certain environments, such as when walking in busy areas or crossing streets, it's important to remain aware of external sounds for safety reasons. Transparency mode allows users to hear the world around them, from conversations to traffic noise, while still enjoying audio content. This creates a safe listening experience where users can enjoy their music or podcasts without becoming isolated from their surroundings, protecting both their hearing and their safety.

A New Standard for Accessibility and Hearing Health

The AirPods Pro 2 represent a revolutionary shift in the way we think about wireless earbuds. Not only are they designed to provide superior sound quality, comfort, and convenience, but they also feature cutting-edge health and accessibility functions that make them invaluable tools for improving hearing and communication. Whether it's through their FDA-approved hearing aid functionality, the 5-minute self-assessment hearing test, or features like Conversation

Awareness and Hearing Protection, the AirPods Pro 2 demonstrate Apple's commitment to making technology more accessible and beneficial to everyone.

The AirPods Pro 2 empower users to take control of their hearing health in a simple and convenient way, providing a personalized, inclusive audio experience that enhances both social interactions and personal well-being. By offering features that improve everyday conversations, protect hearing, and allow for personalized adjustments based on individual needs, Apple has set a new standard for accessibility in personal audio devices. These features are not only a testament to Apple's innovation but also to the growing importance of hearing health and inclusivity in modern technology.

CHAPTER 6

The Global Impact

The release of the AirPods Pro 2 marked a significant turning point not just in the world of personal audio technology, but also in the way hearing aids and accessibility devices are viewed worldwide. Apple's commitment to integrating hearing health features into their products is paving the way for more inclusive technology, helping bridge the gap between high-quality consumer audio and the accessibility needs of millions around the globe. As we explore the global impact of the AirPods Pro 2, we will focus on their accessibility worldwide, the shift in public perception surrounding hearing aids, and Apple's contributions to a healthier future through improved hearing health for all.

In this chapter, we'll delve into the broader implications of the AirPods Pro 2's impact, discussing how Apple is reaching new markets beyond the U.S., helping to reduce the stigma of hearing aids, and promoting hearing health on a global scale. The AirPods Pro 2 have transcended their role as simple wireless earbuds, becoming a vehicle for positive change and expanding access to hearing technology in ways previously unimaginable.

6.1 Accessibility Worldwide: Expanding Reach Beyond the U.S.

Apple has always been known for its global presence, and with the AirPods Pro 2, the company has taken steps to ensure that its innovative hearing health features reach users worldwide. The shift from traditional hearing aids to a more accessible, over-the-counter solution has implications far beyond the U.S. market. The AirPods Pro 2 represent a landmark moment in the accessibility of hearing devices and reflect Apple's broader strategy to improve the quality of life for people all over the world.

Expanding Access to Hearing Aids in Emerging Markets

For years, hearing aids were largely out of reach for many people due to high costs, limited availability, and complicated access to professional healthcare. In many emerging markets, hearing aids were seen as expensive, medically prescribed devices that required visits to audiologists and regular check-ups. This made them inaccessible to a large portion of the population who were dealing with mild to moderate hearing loss. The AirPods Pro 2's FDA approval as over-the-counter hearing aids have the potential to significantly disrupt this paradigm.

By offering a product that can be purchased easily without a prescription, Apple is making hearing assistance more widely available to people who may not have had access to conventional hearing aids. The simplicity of purchasing AirPods Pro 2 and using them as hearing aids reduces logistical barriers and costs, opening up opportunities for those in developing regions who may have previously struggled to find affordable hearing solutions.

The global reach of Apple's ecosystem further amplifies the impact of the AirPods Pro 2. Since Apple products are already widely available in most countries and regions, the AirPods Pro 2's hearing aid functionality can be marketed and distributed easily. This expansion into global markets ensures that people in various regions—whether it's in Asia, Africa, or Latin America—can benefit from the AirPods Pro 2's accessibility features, promoting greater inclusivity and availability of hearing technology to populations that have historically been underserved.

International Partnerships and Regulatory Approvals

Apple's success in global markets also hinges on its ability to navigate the regulatory landscapes of different countries. The AirPods Pro 2's FDA approval as over-the-counter hearing aids was a milestone in the United States, but Apple has also worked to secure similar approvals and certifications in other parts of the world. In the European Union, for example, the AirPods Pro 2 have received the necessary certifications to be sold as medical devices, allowing them to serve as hearing aids across European countries.

Through these international partnerships and regulatory efforts, Apple is able to make the AirPods Pro 2 available to a broader audience, regardless of geographical location. Whether it's the bustling streets of Tokyo or the rural towns of Brazil, the AirPods Pro 2 have the potential to reach millions of people who would benefit from enhanced hearing assistance but have been unable to access traditional hearing aids due to financial, social, or geographical constraints.

6.2 Changing Perceptions: Reducing the Stigma of Hearing Aids

Historically, hearing aids have carried a certain stigma. People with hearing loss often felt embarrassed or self-conscious about wearing hearing aids, which traditionally bulky, visible, and associated with aging or disability. There was also a perception that wearing hearing aids meant admitting to an impairment or weakness, creating barriers for many people to seek help for their hearing issues.

As a result, millions of individuals lived with undiagnosed or untreated hearing loss, often because they didn't want to be labeled or didn't feel comfortable using traditional hearing aids.

The AirPods Pro 2 have played a crucial role in changing this perception by integrating hearing assistance into a sleek, modern, and widely used consumer product. By taking advantage of the same design philosophy that has made AirPods popular worldwide, Apple has created a product that doesn't feel like a medical device. Instead, it is a consumer product that many people already know and love for its ease of use and high-quality audio.

Making Hearing Aids Fashionable and Discreet

One of the key features of the AirPods Pro 2 is their discreet design. Unlike traditional hearing aids, which are often bulky and visibly noticeable, the AirPods Pro 2 are lightweight, small, and blend seamlessly with everyday technology. The sleek design, along with the familiarity of the AirPods brand, helps remove the stigma surrounding hearing aids. These earbuds look like a high-tech accessory, and many users feel more comfortable wearing them because they don't immediately identify the device as a hearing aid. This shift in perception is especially significant for younger generations or those who may be dealing with early stages of hearing loss but don't want to wear something that feels like a medical device.

Apple's focus on creating aesthetically pleasing, high-quality audio products has allowed them to make hearing aids a part of mainstream culture. People who wear AirPods Pro 2 can go about their daily lives without drawing attention to the fact that they are using hearing-enhancement technology. This subtlety has helped normalize the idea of using technology to improve hearing, leading to more people taking the necessary steps to address hearing loss without feeling embarrassed or self-conscious.

Changing the Narrative Around Hearing Loss

By integrating hearing aids into a consumer product like the AirPods Pro 2, Apple is also changing the broader narrative around hearing loss. No longer are hearing aids only for older individuals or those with significant impairment—they are now an accessible solution for people of all ages who want to enhance their hearing experience. The AirPods Pro 2 help normalize hearing loss as a condition that can be managed easily and discreetly, just like using glasses to correct vision or a smartphone to stay connected.

As more people begin using products like the AirPods Pro 2 to address hearing loss, the stigma surrounding hearing aids will likely continue to decrease. The idea that hearing aids are no longer just for those in advanced stages of hearing impairment will encourage individuals to seek out hearing assistance earlier, improving their quality of life and preventing further damage to their hearing.

6.3 A Healthier Future: Promoting Hearing Health Globally

Apple's efforts with the AirPods Pro 2 go beyond just offering a consumer product—they are part of a larger movement to improve hearing health worldwide. As hearing loss becomes a more prevalent issue in aging populations, it is essential to raise awareness about hearing health and promote accessible solutions. Apple's work in this area is helping to change the way we approach hearing health, making it easier for people to monitor and improve their hearing, while also reducing the barriers to access that have traditionally made hearing aids expensive and difficult to obtain.

Raising Awareness About Hearing Loss

Hearing loss is an often-overlooked health issue, despite the fact that it affects millions of people worldwide. According to the World Health Organization (WHO), approximately 1.5

billion people live with some form of hearing loss, and this number is expected to increase as populations age. However, despite the prevalence of hearing loss, many people go undiagnosed or untreated, partly due to a lack of awareness and partly due to the stigma surrounding hearing aids.

Apple's AirPods Pro 2 play an important role in raising awareness about hearing health by offering an easy-to-use, accessible product that encourages users to take an active role in their hearing care. By providing a self-assessment hearing test and FDA-approved hearing aid functionality, Apple is helping users understand the importance of addressing hearing issues early. The simple, accessible approach to hearing care makes it easier for people to monitor their hearing health and seek treatment when necessary.

Encouraging Regular Hearing Health Checks

In addition to the hearing test feature in the AirPods Pro 2, Apple's wider ecosystem of devices (such as the Apple Watch and iPhone) encourages users to prioritize their health in general, with health monitoring features built into these products. The AirPods Pro 2 can be seamlessly integrated into this ecosystem, reminding users to take their hearing health seriously and offering them the tools to do so.

With the AirPods Pro 2, users are empowered to regularly assess their hearing health, which can help them catch potential issues early on. By providing a product that makes hearing health accessible and straightforward, Apple is helping to build a future where hearing loss is addressed more proactively and earlier in life.

Building an Inclusive Future

The AirPods Pro 2 and their hearing health features are part of Apple's broader commitment to creating products that serve a diverse and global population. The company's focus on accessibility ensures that individuals of all ages and backgrounds have the tools they need to manage their hearing health and enjoy high-quality audio experiences. This inclusivity is not just about providing technology—it's about making sure that people from all walks of life have access to the same opportunities to hear and communicate.

Apple's Role in Global Health

Apple's investment in health technology is reshaping the future of healthcare. With the AirPods Pro 2's focus on hearing health, Apple is setting a new standard for what it means to design technology that not only enhances daily life but also contributes to better long-term health. By promoting hearing health on a global scale, Apple is positioning itself as a leader in health and wellness, using its influence and resources to improve lives worldwide.

The AirPods Pro 2's Transformative Impact

The AirPods Pro 2 are much more than just a pair of high-quality wireless earbuds—they are a catalyst for positive change in the world of hearing health and accessibility. Through their accessibility worldwide, their role in reducing the stigma of hearing aids, and their broader contributions to promoting hearing health globally, the AirPods Pro 2 represent a new era of personal technology that prioritizes health, inclusivity, and well-being.

As Apple continues to expand the reach of its products and push the boundaries of what is possible in health technology, the AirPods Pro 2 are setting the stage for a healthier, more inclusive future. By making hearing aids more accessible, raising awareness about hearing health, and providing people with the tools to improve their hearing experience, Apple is changing the way we think about hearing care. The AirPods Pro 2 are just the beginning of what will likely be a long-term movement toward greater accessibility and better health outcomes for millions around the globe.

CHAPTER 7

The Apple Ecosystem Advantage

When Apple introduced the AirPods in 2016, the company didn't just launch a pair of wireless earbuds—it introduced a new standard of seamless integration that has become synonymous with the Apple ecosystem. As part of this ecosystem, the AirPods Pro 2, Apple's most recent iteration of the AirPods line, represent the pinnacle of how well Apple products can work together to offer a unified, intuitive, and user-friendly experience. This chapter explores the Apple ecosystem advantage in relation to the AirPods Pro 2, highlighting their seamless integration with Apple devices, the limitations of using them with non-Apple products, and the exciting future prospects of AirPods Pro 2 and Apple's audio technology as a whole.

In this chapter, we'll dive deep into how the AirPods Pro 2 fit into the larger Apple ecosystem, the advantages this offers users, the limitations they face when using non-Apple devices, and what innovations we might see in future iterations of the AirPods series. Whether you are a long-time Apple user or a newcomer to the ecosystem, understanding these key aspects of the AirPods Pro 2 will deepen your appreciation for how Apple's audio products enhance the overall user experience.

7.1 Seamless Integration with Apple Devices: A Unified Experience

The hallmark of any Apple product is its ability to integrate seamlessly with other devices in the Apple ecosystem. The AirPods Pro 2 take this integration to the next level, offering an experience that feels intuitive, fluid, and designed to work in perfect harmony with all your Apple products. Whether you're using an iPhone, iPad, Mac, or Apple Watch, the AirPods Pro 2 offer an effortless experience that enhances your interactions with each device.

Automatic Pairing and Device Switching

One of the most impressive features of the AirPods Pro 2 is the automatic pairing and device switching that occurs when you use them with Apple devices. The moment you open the case near an Apple device, the AirPods Pro 2 are recognized, and a prompt appears on the screen asking if you'd like to connect. This "one-step" connection process has made AirPods the benchmark for simplicity in Bluetooth devices. The ability to automatically connect to Apple devices without requiring complicated Bluetooth settings or manual intervention makes the AirPods Pro 2 ideal for users who want an effortless experience.

Once paired with an Apple device, the AirPods Pro 2 also feature automatic switching. This means that if you're listening to music on your iPhone and then decide to join a Zoom call on your Mac, the AirPods Pro 2 will automatically switch to the Mac without you needing to do anything. The same goes if you're using your AirPods Pro 2 with your Apple Watch to listen to music while exercising, and then want to take a call on your iPhone—you don't need to manually disconnect and reconnect the earbuds. The AirPods Pro 2 seamlessly detect which device you're using and shift between them automatically, providing a frictionless experience.

This level of integration is a key part of Apple's broader vision of making its devices work together effortlessly. Apple products aren't just individual devices—they are designed to complement and enhance each other, creating a unified experience that other tech ecosystems simply can't match.

iCloud Integration for Multiple Device Access

Another standout feature of the AirPods Pro 2's integration with the Apple ecosystem is iCloud. Once paired with one

Apple device, your AirPods Pro 2 will be available for automatic use across all of your Apple devices that are signed into the same iCloud account. For example, if you pair your AirPods Pro 2 with your iPhone, they will automatically be accessible on your iPad, Mac, Apple Watch, and even Apple TV without needing to manually pair each device.

This cross-device accessibility is especially useful for users who work or study across multiple Apple devices. Imagine you're listening to a podcast on your iPhone, then decide to switch to your MacBook for work. With iCloud integration, your AirPods Pro 2 will instantly switch to your Mac, allowing you to pick up where you left off with no need to reconnect or manually adjust the settings.

This level of integration streamlines the user experience, making it easy to stay connected and keep the flow of your daily tasks moving forward without interruption. Whether you're working, learning, or relaxing, the AirPods Pro 2 provide a seamless connection to all your Apple devices.

Spatial Audio and Apple's Proprietary Features

The AirPods Pro 2's integration with Apple's spatial audio technology is another area where the ecosystem shines. Spatial audio, with dynamic head tracking, offers a 3D audio experience that makes media consumption far more immersive. Whether you're watching a movie on your iPhone or listening to music through Apple Music, spatial audio creates a surround-sound experience that adapts as you move your head, making it feel like the sound is coming from all around you.

The dynamic head tracking and the personalized spatial audio features of the AirPods Pro 2 are powered by the Apple ecosystem's built-in sensors, including the iPhone's gyroscope and accelerometer. These sensors work together to provide a more immersive and personalized sound experience, ensuring that audio is optimized for the user's head movements and hearing profile.

For users of Apple services like Apple Music, Apple TV+, or Apple Podcasts, this experience is enhanced even further. The tight integration between the AirPods Pro 2 and Apple's content services ensures that spatial audio and dynamic head tracking work flawlessly, creating an experience that is optimized specifically for Apple users.

7.2 Limitations with Non-Apple Devices: What You Might Miss

While the AirPods Pro 2 excel within the Apple ecosystem, they do have limitations when it comes to compatibility with non-Apple devices. Though the AirPods Pro 2 are Bluetooth-enabled and can be used with many other devices, they don't offer the same level of functionality and convenience when paired with devices outside the Apple ecosystem. Here's a closer look at what you might miss when using the AirPods Pro 2 with non-Apple devices.

Limited Automatic Device Switching

One of the most noticeable features you'll miss when using the AirPods Pro 2 with non-Apple devices is automatic device switching. As discussed earlier, when used within the Apple ecosystem, the AirPods Pro 2 will seamlessly switch between devices without any input from the user. However, this functionality does not extend to non-Apple devices. If you're using an AirPods Pro 2 with a Windows PC, Android phone, or other Bluetooth-enabled device, you will need to manually disconnect from one device and reconnect to another.

While Bluetooth pairing itself is still simple and easy to use, this lack of automatic switching can be a hassle, especially if you're used to the convenience offered by Apple devices. Users who work with multiple devices throughout the day may find it frustrating to constantly manage their connections when using AirPods Pro 2 with non-Apple devices.

Limited Access to Apple-Specific Features

While the AirPods Pro 2 will work with non-Apple devices for basic audio functions, many of the proprietary features Apple offers, such as spatial audio, Siri integration, and seamless iCloud syncing, are limited or unavailable when used with non-Apple devices.

Spatial Audio: While the AirPods Pro 2's spatial audio feature will work with some third-party content, like certain videos or games that support 3D audio, it's best experienced with Apple's native apps. Apple Music, Apple TV+, and other Apple services are fully optimized to support spatial audio, but non-Apple content or devices may not offer the same immersive experience.

Siri Integration: Siri, Apple's virtual assistant, is fully integrated into the AirPods Pro 2, allowing users to control music, make calls, set reminders, and more with voice commands. However, this feature is unavailable when paired with non-Apple devices. Android users, for instance, won't be able to use Siri with their AirPods Pro 2. Instead, they'll have to rely on other voice assistants, like Google Assistant, which may not offer the same seamless experience as Siri.

No Seamless Multi-Device Syncing

Without iCloud integration, non-Apple devices don't offer the same level of synchronization as Apple devices do. The ability to automatically switch between devices and stay connected across multiple platforms is a key benefit of the Apple ecosystem, but when using AirPods Pro 2 with non-Apple devices, users will need to manually pair and switch between devices each time they want to use the AirPods with a different product.

This lack of seamless multi-device syncing can be a frustration for users who rely on the ease of switching between their phone, tablet, and laptop throughout the day. While you can use the AirPods Pro 2 with a non-Apple device, you miss out on one of their standout features: effortless integration with other Apple devices.

7.3 Future Prospects: What's Next for AirPods Pro 2

As technology continues to evolve at a rapid pace, it's natural to wonder what the future holds for the AirPods Pro series, especially with the recent release of the AirPods Pro 2. Apple has set the bar high with these earbuds, integrating advanced features like spatial audio, Active Noise Cancellation (ANC), and personalized hearing health, but there's always room for improvement and innovation. Let's look at some exciting possibilities for the future of the AirPods Pro 2 and the next generation of wireless earbuds from Apple.

Improved Integration with Health and Wellness Features

Given Apple's growing focus on health and wellness, it's likely that future AirPods models will see even deeper integration with health monitoring features. The AirPods Pro 2 already include features like hearing health assessments and FDA-approved hearing aid functionality, but future versions could expand on this with more advanced health tracking. Apple might integrate sensors for monitoring heart rate, blood oxygen levels, and even body temperature through the AirPods, providing a comprehensive health monitoring system that goes beyond hearing health.

Better Battery Life and Charging Innovations

Battery life is always a focal point for any wearable device, and the AirPods Pro 2 have made notable strides in this area, offering up to six hours of listening time on a single charge. However, there's always room for improvement. Future AirPods models could see even longer battery life, especially as Apple continues to refine its power management systems and the efficiency of chips like the H2. Additionally, advancements in charging technology, such as faster wireless charging or even longer-lasting battery materials, could extend the time between charges, making the AirPods even more convenient for users on the go.

Further Advancements in Active Noise Cancellation

Active Noise Cancellation (ANC) is one of the key features of the AirPods Pro 2, and while the current version offers impressive performance, Apple will likely continue to improve this technology in future models. Expect even better ANC performance, particularly in environments with dynamic or unpredictable noise, such as on an airplane or in a crowded café. Apple could leverage machine learning and more advanced algorithms to create an even more adaptive ANC experience that more effectively isolates unwanted sounds while preserving audio quality.

Augmented Reality (AR) Integration

With the rapid advancements in augmented reality, it's possible that future iterations of the AirPods Pro could feature AR functionality, turning the earbuds into a key component of an immersive, hands-free AR experience. Imagine using the AirPods Pro in conjunction with AR glasses or your iPhone to navigate through a virtual environment, providing audio cues and enhancing the experience of digital content.

Expanded Integration with Non-Apple Devices

Although the AirPods Pro 2 are currently best experienced within the Apple ecosystem, Apple may eventually improve their compatibility with non-Apple devices. By introducing more universal features and optimizations, Apple could make it easier for users of Android devices, Windows PCs, and other platforms to enjoy a similar level of integration with the AirPods Pro 2. This could include the addition of certain features like automatic switching, spatial audio, and deeper voice assistant integration for non-Apple devices.

The AirPods Pro 2 stand as a testament to Apple's ability to create innovative, high-performance products that seamlessly integrate into the Apple ecosystem. Through features like automatic device switching, spatial audio, and personalized hearing health, the AirPods Pro 2 offer a superior user experience for Apple customers. While there are limitations when using them with non-Apple devices, the AirPods Pro 2's unmatched functionality within the Apple ecosystem ensures that they remain a top choice for users invested in Apple's products and services.

Looking ahead, Apple's commitment to innovation means the future of AirPods is incredibly exciting. Whether it's improving battery life, integrating more health features, or expanding their compatibility across devices, the AirPods Pro 2 represent just the beginning of what's possible in the world of wearable audio technology. For those already embedded in the Apple ecosystem, the AirPods Pro 2 offer an unmatched listening experience that is only going to improve as Apple continues to push the envelope in the years to come.

CHAPTER 8

User Experiences and Testimonials

The true value of any product, especially one as innovative as the AirPods Pro 2, often lies in the experiences of the people who use them. While Apple's marketing and product specifications are impressive, it's the real stories from everyday users, expert opinions from audiologists and technologists, and feedback from online communities that truly highlight how the AirPods Pro 2 make a meaningful difference in people's lives. This chapter delves into the personal experiences, expert assessments, and community feedback to offer a comprehensive look at the impact the AirPods Pro 2 have had on users around the world.

From individuals with hearing impairments to audiophiles seeking high-quality sound, the AirPods Pro 2 have found their place in a wide range of lifestyles. Let's explore the real-world stories, professional opinions, and online discussions that provide a full picture of the AirPods Pro 2's performance, benefits, and some potential drawbacks.

8.1 Real Stories: How Users Have Benefited from AirPods Pro 2

The AirPods Pro 2 are a game-changer for a variety of users, each with unique needs and preferences. From casual listeners to those seeking hearing assistance, the AirPods Pro 2 have made a tangible difference in the daily lives of many. Here, we'll explore a few real stories from AirPods Pro 2 users who have benefited from the product in different ways.

Improving Hearing Health for the Elderly

Many users who have mild to moderate hearing loss have found that the AirPods Pro 2 provide an excellent, affordable alternative to traditional hearing aids. For example, Susan, a 68-year-old retiree from Florida, shared how the AirPods Pro 2 helped her enjoy a better quality of life. "I've been struggling with hearing loss for a few years, but I didn't want to wear traditional hearing aids—they felt bulky, and I didn't want to feel like I was 'old.' But with the AirPods Pro 2, I don't have to worry about that. They look like regular earbuds, and they work just like hearing aids for me."

Susan went on to explain how the Adaptive Audio feature, combined with the FDA-approved hearing aid functionality, helped her engage more actively in conversations. "Now, when I'm at family gatherings, I don't miss out on conversations. I can adjust the audio amplification based on how loud it is, and it feels like I'm hearing everything clearly, just like I used to."

For Susan and others like her, the AirPods Pro 2 have bridged the gap between hearing assistance and everyday tech, allowing users to benefit from advanced hearing features without the stigma traditionally associated with hearing aids.

An Athlete's Perspective: Enhanced Focus During Workouts

Another user, Tim, a professional marathon runner, found that the AirPods Pro 2 were not only great for listening to music but also crucial for staying focused during his training sessions. "As an athlete, I need to stay focused and block out distractions. The AirPods Pro 2's Active Noise Cancellation feature was a game-changer for me. I used to be distracted by other runners, traffic, and noise during my runs, but now I can fully immerse myself in my music and concentrate on my pace."

Tim explained that the customizable fit and the comfort of the AirPods Pro 2 allowed him to wear them for hours during his training without discomfort. "The ergonomic design fits snugly, and I never have to worry about them falling out during intense workouts, whether I'm running or cycling. It's not just about blocking noise; it's about being able to engage in my training without distractions."

Athletes and fitness enthusiasts like Tim have found that the AirPods Pro 2 enhance focus and performance by providing an immersive, uninterrupted experience during exercise. Whether it's music for motivation or simply blocking out external noise, the AirPods Pro 2 have become an indispensable part of many fitness routines.

Young Professionals: The Convenience of Work and Play

For professionals like Mark, a 35-year-old project manager, the AirPods Pro 2 offer a seamless transition between work and leisure. "I'm on calls all day, and I've got to be on top of my game during meetings. But once I'm done with work, I want to unwind with music or a podcast. The AirPods Pro 2 let me do both without any hassle."

Mark praises the AirPods Pro 2 for their effortless device switching and their ability to block out background noise during virtual meetings. "The automatic switching between my MacBook and iPhone is amazing. If I get a call while I'm on a Zoom meeting, I don't even have to touch anything— my AirPods just switch to the phone seamlessly. And when I'm listening to music after work, the sound quality is incredible. I love the clarity and depth of the bass."

For young professionals, the AirPods Pro 2 have become the ultimate multitasking tool, offering smooth transitions between work, meetings, calls, and personal entertainment.

8.2 Expert Opinions: Audiologists and Technologists Weigh In

While user experiences are invaluable in understanding the real-world benefits of a product, expert opinions from audiologists, sound engineers, and technologists offer a deeper understanding of how the AirPods Pro 2 stack up against other devices on the market. In this section, we'll examine insights from professionals in the field of audio and hearing health to provide a well-rounded perspective on the AirPods Pro 2's performance.

Audiologists on Hearing Aid Functionality

Dr. Linda Hargrave, an audiologist with over 20 years of experience in hearing healthcare, notes that the AirPods Pro 2's FDA-approved hearing aid functionality is a significant advancement in the accessibility of hearing devices. "For years, hearing aids have been seen as a niche medical device for those with severe hearing loss, often requiring prescriptions and professional fittings. What Apple has done with the AirPods Pro 2 is democratize hearing assistance, making it available over-the-counter for people with mild to moderate hearing loss. This is an exciting development because it lowers the barrier to entry for people who might have otherwise gone untreated."

Dr. Hargrave emphasizes that while the AirPods Pro 2 may not replace a custom-fitted hearing aid for those with severe hearing loss, they are an excellent solution for many people with hearing issues. "The amplification and sound processing capabilities are impressive, and the ability to personalize sound settings through the hearing test is a fantastic feature. It's particularly beneficial for individuals who are starting to notice hearing changes but don't yet need a full-fledged hearing aid."

Technologists Discussing Audio Quality

James Miller, a technologist and sound engineer, shares his take on the AirPods Pro 2's sound quality, which he finds to be exceptional for wireless earbuds. "When it comes to wireless earbuds, the AirPods Pro 2 are as close as you can get to studio-quality sound in a portable device. Apple has done an outstanding job of optimizing the H2 chip to handle complex sound profiles, making the audio dynamic and immersive. The integration of spatial audio is particularly impressive, offering a 3D sound experience that adapts to your movements, whether you're watching movies, playing games, or listening to music."

James notes that the custom drivers in the AirPods Pro 2 provide clarity and balance across a wide range of frequencies. "The bass is deep without being overwhelming, the mids are rich and detailed, and the highs are crisp and clear. Whether you're listening to high-fidelity music or engaging with immersive content, the AirPods Pro 2 deliver a superb audio experience."

Battery Life and Efficiency

Another area where experts have praised the AirPods Pro 2 is their battery efficiency. According to battery technology expert Dr. Emily Peters, "Apple has made significant strides in power management with the AirPods Pro 2. The six-hour battery life on a single charge, coupled with the charging case that offers 30 hours of total usage, is impressive. This efficiency is especially important for users who rely on their earbuds for long periods, such as during travel or extended work sessions."

Dr. Peters also highlights the role of the H2 chip in improving energy consumption. "The H2 chip not only boosts performance but also optimizes power usage. This results in longer listening times and faster charging without compromising on audio quality or functionality. It's a smart move by Apple, as users are constantly seeking longer battery life in their portable devices."

8.3 Community Feedback: Insights from Online Forums and Reviews

In addition to expert opinions and user stories, online forums and reviews offer a wealth of insights from real-world users discussing both the pros and cons of the AirPods Pro 2. These platforms provide a more candid, varied perspective on the product, with feedback ranging from enthusiastic praise to constructive criticism.

Positive Reviews: Enhanced Audio, Comfort, and Usability

Many users across online communities like Reddit and the Apple Support Forum have praised the AirPods Pro 2 for their enhanced audio experience, comfort, and usability. One Reddit user shared, "I was already a fan of the original AirPods Pro, but the AirPods Pro 2 are a whole new level. The noise cancellation is unbelievable, and the sound is so much richer. Plus, the personalized hearing test feature is a game-changer for me—I can actually hear music the way it was meant to be heard again."

Another reviewer on the Apple Support Forum commented, "I use my AirPods Pro 2 for everything—work meetings, listening to music, and even watching movies. The automatic switching between devices is so convenient, and I never have to worry about reconnecting when I switch from my iPhone to my MacBook."

These positive reviews highlight the convenience, comfort, and functionality of the AirPods Pro 2, especially for users who are already within the Apple ecosystem. For many, the AirPods Pro 2 have become a daily essential, enhancing productivity, entertainment, and even personal health.

Constructive Criticism: Limitations with Non-Apple Devices and Durability Concerns

While most reviews are positive, some users have pointed out limitations when using the AirPods Pro 2 with non-Apple devices. One user on Reddit noted, "I love my AirPods Pro 2, but I have trouble switching between my Windows PC and my phone. I have to manually disconnect from one device and reconnect to the other, which isn't as seamless as when I use them with my MacBook or iPhone."

Durability has also been mentioned as a concern by a few users. "I've had my AirPods Pro 2 for about six months, and while the sound quality is still great, I've noticed some wear and tear on the case. The hinge doesn't feel as sturdy as it once did, and I'm worried about it breaking eventually," wrote one reviewer on the Apple Support Forum. While this feedback is less common, it does offer valuable insight for potential buyers, especially those concerned about long-term durability.

Suggestions for Improvement

Several users have offered suggestions for future improvements. One consistent suggestion involves enhancing the customization of noise cancellation. "It would be great if we could adjust the noise cancellation levels manually. Sometimes I want a little noise reduction, but not complete isolation. A customizable slider would make the experience even better," said one user on Reddit.

Others have asked for further improvements to battery life, especially for users who are on the go for extended periods. "Six hours of battery life is great, but I would love to see Apple push this to eight hours or more, especially for people who use their AirPods Pro 2 during long flights or commutes," wrote a user on an online review site.

The AirPods Pro 2 have had a profound impact on users worldwide, improving their ability to enjoy high-quality sound, enhance their hearing, and engage in daily activities more seamlessly. From personal stories of improved hearing health to expert opinions on the technical aspects of the device, it's clear that the AirPods Pro 2 are making a real difference. The product's seamless integration within the Apple ecosystem, its performance across a wide range of use cases, and its positive reception from users and professionals alike suggest that the AirPods Pro 2 are more than just a pair of earbuds—they are a step toward more accessible, immersive, and healthy living through technology.

While the AirPods Pro 2 are not without their limitations, especially when used with non-Apple devices, their overall impact on accessibility, sound quality, and hearing health is undeniable. As Apple continues to innovate and refine its audio technology, the AirPods Pro 2 stand as a benchmark for what's possible in the realm of personal audio devices. The feedback from users and experts alike points to a bright future for the AirPods Pro 2 and similar products in Apple's lineup, promising continued advancements in hearing technology, comfort, and integration across all Apple devices.

CHAPTER 9

Troubleshooting and Maintenance

The AirPods Pro 2 are among the most advanced wireless earbuds on the market, delivering an unparalleled combination of sound quality, noise cancellation, and advanced features. However, as with any piece of technology, there are times when issues arise. Whether it's connectivity problems, issues with sound quality, or difficulties with charging, understanding how to troubleshoot and maintain your AirPods Pro 2 is essential for ensuring that they continue to perform at their best.

In this chapter, we'll walk you through some of the most common issues AirPods Pro 2 users face, how to troubleshoot them, and provide practical maintenance tips to keep your earbuds in top shape. We'll also cover when it's appropriate to seek professional help, including how to navigate warranty and support options. By the end of this chapter, you'll have all the tools you need to keep your AirPods Pro 2 working smoothly for years to come.

9.1 Common Issues and Solutions: What to Do When Things Go Wrong

Despite the advanced technology behind the AirPods Pro 2, like any other electronic device, they can occasionally encounter problems. Fortunately, many common issues can be resolved quickly and easily with a few troubleshooting steps. Below are some of the most frequently reported issues with the AirPods Pro 2, along with solutions to help you get them back in working order.

1. Connectivity Issues: AirPods Won't Pair or Connect

One of the most common issues users experience with Bluetooth devices, including AirPods Pro 2, is difficulty connecting them to devices. If you're having trouble pairing your AirPods Pro 2, here's what to do:

Check Bluetooth Settings: Ensure that Bluetooth is turned on in the device you are trying to connect to. For iPhone users, swipe into the Control Center and verify that the Bluetooth icon is active. For non-Apple devices, go into the device's settings and check the Bluetooth status.

Forget and Reconnect: If your AirPods Pro 2 have been paired with the device before but are not connecting, try forgetting the AirPods from the Bluetooth settings of your device. Once you've removed them, go through the pairing process again by opening the case near the device and tapping the prompt to connect.

Reset the AirPods Pro 2: If the above steps don't work, try resetting your AirPods Pro 2. To do this, open the AirPods Pro 2 case, press and hold the button on the back of the case for at least 15 seconds, or until the status light flashes amber and then white. This will restore the AirPods to their factory settings, allowing you to pair them from scratch.

Software Update: Ensure that the device you are connecting to is running the latest version of its operating system. Sometimes, connectivity issues are caused by software bugs that are resolved through updates. For iPhone users, go to Settings > General > Software Update.

2. Sound Quality Problems: Low Volume or Distorted Sound

If you're experiencing low volume or distorted sound while using your AirPods Pro 2, several things might be causing the issue. Try these troubleshooting steps:

Check the Volume Settings: Sometimes, the issue is simply that the volume on your device or within the audio app is too low. Adjust the volume both on your device and the AirPods Pro 2 to see if the problem resolves.

Check the Ear Tips: If the sound quality is muffled or distorted, ensure that you are using the correct size of ear tips for a secure fit. AirPods Pro 2 come with multiple ear tip sizes, and a poor seal can result in low-quality sound and reduced noise isolation. Use the ear tip fit test available in the settings to check the fit.

Enable or Adjust Active Noise Cancellation (ANC): If you are experiencing distortion or reduced sound quality, the ANC feature might be malfunctioning. Go into your device's settings and turn ANC off and on again. Alternatively, you can use Transparency Mode to see if the sound quality improves.

Clean the AirPods Pro 2: Dirt or debris blocking the speaker grilles can cause muffled sound or distortion. Use a dry, soft-bristled brush or a microfiber cloth to clean the openings gently. Be careful not to push dirt further inside.

Reset the AirPods Pro 2: As a last resort, resetting the AirPods can help solve sound quality issues. This will erase any saved settings and pairings, so you'll need to reconnect the AirPods to your devices afterward.

3. Charging Problems: AirPods Not Charging or Poor Battery Life

If your AirPods Pro 2 aren't charging properly or the battery drains quickly, try these solutions:

Check the Charging Cable and Case: Inspect the USB-C cable and charging port for any visible damage. If the cable is damaged, it may not be providing power to the case or the AirPods. Try using a different cable or charging another device with the same cable to confirm whether the issue lies with the cable.

Clean the Charging Contacts: Dirt or debris on the charging contacts inside the case or on the AirPods can prevent proper charging. Gently clean the charging ports and connectors with a soft, dry cloth to remove any buildup.

Check the Charging Case Battery: If the AirPods are not charging properly, the issue may lie with the case itself. To check if the case has charge, place the AirPods back inside and check the status light. If the case is not charging, try plugging it into a different power source to ensure it's getting the proper power.

Reset and Recharge: If the AirPods still won't charge, try resetting them as described earlier. After resetting, place the AirPods Pro 2 back in the case and check if they start charging.

4. Microphone Issues: Problems with Calls and Siri

Another common issue is problems with the AirPods Pro 2's microphone, particularly during phone calls or when using Siri. If the other person can't hear you clearly or if Siri isn't responding well, try the following:

Check for Blockages: Make sure that the microphones on the AirPods are clean and free from dirt or debris. Clean the microphones with a dry, soft brush or a microfiber cloth to ensure clear sound input.

Toggle Between ANC and Transparency Mode: Sometimes, switching between Active Noise Cancellation (ANC) and Transparency Mode can help with microphone clarity. Try switching modes to see if there is an improvement in voice clarity during calls.

Test with Another Device: If the microphone is still not working properly, try using the AirPods Pro 2 with a different device. This will help determine if the issue is with the AirPods or the device itself.

Update Software: Ensure your iPhone or iPad has the latest software update. A software bug could be causing issues with the microphone functionality.

5. No Sound in One Ear

If you're experiencing no sound in one ear, the problem is likely a connection issue or a malfunction in the AirPods. Here's how to resolve it:

Check Bluetooth Connection: Ensure that both AirPods are connected properly. If you see that one AirPod is not connected, try disconnecting and reconnecting them through your Bluetooth settings.

Clean the AirPods: Sometimes, earwax or debris can block the sound from reaching one of the AirPods. Clean the AirPods thoroughly, paying special attention to the speaker grills and microphone openings.

Reset the AirPods Pro 2: If all else fails, resetting the AirPods Pro 2 is a quick way to solve many issues. After resetting, check if the sound comes back in both ears.

9.2 Keeping Your AirPods Pro 2 in Top Shape: Care Tips and Best Practices

Maintaining the condition of your AirPods Pro 2 is crucial for ensuring long-term functionality. Proper care and regular maintenance will keep your earbuds working optimally for years. Here are some essential tips to keep your AirPods Pro 2 in top shape:

1. Cleaning and Hygiene

Since the AirPods Pro 2 are worn in your ears, keeping them clean is essential for both hygiene and performance. To keep your AirPods Pro 2 in the best condition, follow these cleaning guidelines:

Clean the Ear Tips Regularly: Remove the silicone ear tips and wash them gently with water and mild soap. Make sure to dry them completely before reattaching them to the AirPods Pro 2.

Clean the Speaker Grills: Use a soft, dry brush or a microfiber cloth to gently clean the speaker grills and microphones. Avoid using any liquids or cleaning agents directly on the AirPods.

Wipe the Case: Regularly wipe the charging case with a microfiber cloth to keep it free of dust, fingerprints, and grime. Be careful not to allow moisture to get inside the charging ports.

Use a Charging Dock: If you want to protect the charging case from dirt and damage, consider using a protective case or charging dock for your AirPods Pro 2.

2. Store Them Properly

When you're not using your AirPods Pro 2, always store them in their charging case. This protects the earbuds from dust, dirt, and accidental damage. The charging case also ensures that the AirPods Pro 2 remain charged and ready to go when you need them. Avoid leaving your AirPods Pro 2 out in direct sunlight or in extremely hot or cold environments, as this can damage the battery life.

3. Keep the Firmware Updated

Just like with other Apple devices, keeping your AirPods Pro 2 firmware updated is essential for ensuring that they run smoothly and benefit from the latest features. AirPods Pro 2 automatically update their firmware when placed in their charging case and connected to an iPhone, so ensure that your AirPods are updated regularly.

4. Use with Compatible Devices

To get the most out of your AirPods Pro 2, it's best to use them with Apple devices. The AirPods Pro 2 are designed to work seamlessly with the Apple ecosystem, providing features like automatic device switching, iCloud syncing, and spatial audio. While they do work with non-Apple devices, using them with Apple devices ensures you have access to the full range of features.

5. Monitor Battery Health

While the battery life of the AirPods Pro 2 is impressive, it's important to keep an eye on the battery health over time. Regularly charge your AirPods and the charging case, and avoid letting them completely drain before recharging. Additionally, if you notice a significant drop in battery life, it may be time to consider a battery replacement through Apple's support services.

9.3 When to Seek Professional Help: Understanding Warranty and Support Options

Despite your best efforts to maintain your AirPods Pro 2, there may be times when professional help is needed. Whether it's a hardware issue, a software bug, or something else that can't be fixed through troubleshooting, understanding your warranty and support options is essential for getting your AirPods back in working condition.

1. Warranty Coverage

The AirPods Pro 2 come with a one-year limited warranty that covers defects in materials and workmanship. If your AirPods are experiencing issues that are covered under the warranty, Apple will repair or replace them at no charge. However, the warranty does not cover accidental damage or misuse, such as dropping the AirPods in water or damaging them physically.

CHAPTER 10

The Future of AirPods Pro

The AirPods series, particularly the AirPods Pro, has become a flagship product in Apple's ecosystem, redefining how people listen to music, engage in phone calls, and interact with their devices. As of the release of the AirPods Pro 2, these earbuds have come a long way from their initial introduction in 2016, offering impressive sound quality, noise cancellation, personalized audio features, and seamless integration with Apple's devices. However, given the rapid pace of technological advancement, the future of AirPods Pro promises to be even more transformative.

In this chapter, we will take an in-depth look at what the future holds for AirPods Pro, focusing on anticipated features in upcoming models, the role that artificial intelligence (AI) and machine learning may play in shaping smarter listening experiences, and the broader vision of how AirPods Pro will evolve in a post-2025 world. With an eye on the horizon, we'll explore the exciting possibilities that lie ahead for this iconic device.

10.1 Anticipated Features in Upcoming Models: What Could Be Next?

Apple has consistently pushed the boundaries of innovation with its AirPods series, and the future of the AirPods Pro holds even more potential. With each new iteration, Apple has added features that enhance both functionality and user experience, such as improved Active Noise Cancellation (ANC), longer battery life, better sound quality, and the introduction of spatial audio. As we look to the next decade, several anticipated features could further redefine the AirPods Pro.

1. Enhanced Active Noise Cancellation (ANC)

Active Noise Cancellation is one of the standout features of the AirPods Pro, and it's likely that future models will offer even more advanced ANC. While the current AirPods Pro 2 already feature remarkable ANC capabilities, there is always room for improvement in this area. Apple may leverage more advanced microphones, sensors, and algorithms to create even more effective noise cancellation, especially in environments with highly variable background noise, like crowded airports or busy city streets.

It's possible that future AirPods models will use adaptive ANC that responds more dynamically to the wearer's environment. For instance, the ANC could become more aggressive when detecting higher levels of noise or reduce power when in quieter environments, all while maintaining optimal sound quality. In addition, Apple may integrate a more granular control system for ANC, allowing users to fine-tune how much background noise they want to block.

2. Improved Battery Life and Faster Charging

As users demand longer battery life from their devices, Apple is expected to continue refining its battery technology. The AirPods Pro 2 already boast six hours of listening time with ANC active, but there's room to extend that, especially considering how AirPods are used throughout the day for both work and entertainment.

Apple may use more energy-efficient chips and components, as well as advanced power management systems, to further extend battery life without compromising performance. Additionally, faster charging technology could allow users to achieve more playtime in a shorter period, making the AirPods Pro even more convenient for those always on the go.

3. Advanced Health Monitoring Capabilities

Given Apple's focus on health and wellness through devices like the Apple Watch, it's likely that future AirPods models will see enhanced health features. The AirPods Pro 2 already have some health-related functionality, such as personalized hearing profiles through the built-in hearing test, but future iterations could take this even further.

For instance, future AirPods could be equipped with additional sensors that monitor other aspects of health, such as heart rate, body temperature, or blood oxygen levels. With these added sensors, AirPods could offer more comprehensive health tracking capabilities, much like the Apple Watch. This would provide a unique opportunity to gather more data on your body's response to various environments and activities, allowing for a more integrated approach to wellness.

4. Integration with Augmented Reality (AR)

Apple has made significant strides in the augmented reality space, particularly with the development of the ARKit framework and rumored AR glasses. In the future, AirPods Pro could become an integral part of the AR experience. For example, spatial audio and real-time environmental mapping could provide a more immersive AR experience, where sound adjusts dynamically based on your virtual surroundings.

The ability to seamlessly integrate AirPods Pro with AR content could transform the way people engage with both virtual and real-world environments. Imagine walking through a city with AR glasses and receiving directional audio cues through your AirPods, or interacting with virtual objects that produce sounds that seem to come from specific locations in space. This could revolutionize how AR is used in gaming, navigation, education, and even work environments.

5. Customizable Sound Profiles for Individual Users

As AI and machine learning continue to evolve, future AirPods could include even more advanced sound personalization features. The current iteration of AirPods Pro allows for a hearing test to create a personalized audio experience, but future versions could take this further by automatically adjusting sound quality based on the user's preferences, environment, and even the type of content being consumed.

For example, AirPods could learn the user's preferred audio settings over time and automatically adjust the sound to fit different activities. For a user who enjoys bass-heavy music, AirPods could tweak the audio profile to enhance low-end frequencies, while for podcasts or audiobooks, the treble and midrange could be accentuated for clarity.

6. More Advanced Integration with Smart Home Devices

As the smart home ecosystem continues to expand, future versions of AirPods Pro could serve as more effective hubs for controlling smart devices. Currently, Siri allows users to control devices like lights, thermostats, and smart speakers, but with more advanced features, AirPods Pro could become an even more integral part of the smart home experience.

For example, AirPods Pro could be equipped with sensors that detect when users are home or approaching their house and automatically adjust the environment to their preferences—activating the thermostat, dimming the lights, or even opening the garage door—all through a simple voice command or automated setting.

10.2 The Role of AI and Machine Learning: Smarter Listening Experiences

Artificial intelligence and machine learning are two of the most transformative technologies of the 21st century, and they are already playing a significant role in shaping the future of personal audio devices like the AirPods Pro 2. In future models, we can expect even more advanced applications of AI and machine learning to create smarter, more personalized listening experiences.

1. Real-Time Sound Adjustments

AI and machine learning could allow AirPods Pro to make real-time sound adjustments based on external factors such as ambient noise, user behavior, and the type of media being consumed. For example, if you're in a crowded environment, the AI could automatically increase ANC or adjust the volume to compensate for the surrounding noise. Similarly, if the AirPods detect that you're listening to a podcast or audiobook, the sound profile could be adjusted for clarity and intelligibility, ensuring the best experience based on the content.

2. Advanced Speech Recognition for Personalized Interaction

One of the areas where AI could significantly improve the AirPods Pro 2 experience is in speech recognition. Currently, Siri allows for voice commands, but future versions of AirPods could integrate more advanced voice recognition that understands context, intent, and even the speaker's mood. With this level of sophistication, AirPods could act as more intuitive personal assistants, capable of handling more complex tasks based on verbal cues.

For instance, if you mention that you're heading to a meeting, Siri could automatically silence notifications, adjust the sound settings, and even send a message to let others know you're unavailable. The AirPods could also better understand your voice commands in noisy environments, filtering out irrelevant background noise and focusing on the user's speech for more accurate responses.

3. Context-Aware Listening

AI could also make AirPods Pro even more context-aware, adjusting features like noise cancellation, transparency mode, and volume based on where you are and what you're doing. For instance, if you're walking through a park, the AI might switch to a more open transparency mode to let in more ambient sound. If you enter a quiet library, it could automatically ramp up noise cancellation for a more immersive listening experience.

As the AI becomes more attuned to individual preferences and routines, it could create an entirely personalized and intuitive listening experience without the user having to interact with settings or make manual adjustments.

10.3 AirPods Pro in a Post-2025 World: Envisioning the Next Decade

As we look to the future of AirPods Pro, the next decade promises to bring significant advancements that will revolutionize the way we use personal audio devices. In the post-2025 world, AirPods Pro could become even more deeply integrated into the daily lives of users, not just as a tool for listening to music or taking calls, but as a central component of a larger, more immersive digital ecosystem.

1. Integration with Augmented and Virtual Reality

By 2025 and beyond, augmented and virtual reality could become mainstream technologies, and AirPods Pro could evolve to become critical components of the AR/VR ecosystem. The seamless connection between AR glasses and AirPods could provide a truly immersive experience, with spatial audio and haptic feedback combining to create virtual environments that feel incredibly real.

Imagine attending a virtual meeting where the AirPods deliver spatialized audio from different directions based on the virtual layout of the room. Or consider playing a VR game where the sounds of the environment—footsteps, weather, background noise—are dynamically adjusted based on your head movements, creating an incredibly immersive experience that goes beyond what we currently experience with traditional headphones.

2. Advanced Health Applications

The next decade could also see AirPods Pro become even more integrated into the realm of health and wellness. With AI and sensors becoming more advanced, future AirPods models could track a wide range of biometric data beyond just heart rate and hearing levels. They could monitor stress levels, hydration, posture, and even emotional states, offering real-time feedback and suggestions to help users maintain overall health.

For example, AirPods Pro could analyze a user's heart rate variability or stress levels based on vocal tone or physical activity, offering suggestions for relaxation or adjustments to daily routines. Combined with the health tracking capabilities of the Apple Watch and other Apple devices, AirPods could play a pivotal role in managing physical and mental well-being.

CONCLUSION

The Evolution and Future of AirPods Pro 2

The journey we have taken through this book has explored the remarkable evolution of Apple's AirPods Pro 2 and the impact they've had not only on audio technology but also on how we experience and interact with the world around us. From their initial introduction to their current state as one of the most sophisticated audio devices on the market, the AirPods Pro 2 have established themselves as a symbol of innovation, accessibility, and versatility. This conclusion will encapsulate the key insights from each chapter while providing a final reflection on the AirPods Pro 2's place in the world of technology and what the future holds for these groundbreaking devices.

A Revolutionary Leap in Audio Technology

When Apple first released the original AirPods in 2016, they marked a significant shift in how we perceive wireless audio. With the AirPods Pro 2, Apple has continued to build on that foundation, transforming the product into a full-fledged audio and health assistant. Through an enhanced design, superior sound quality, and next-level features like Active Noise Cancellation (ANC), Adaptive Audio, and

Personalized Spatial Audio, the AirPods Pro 2 have revolutionized not just what we hear but how we hear.

The sound quality, in particular, has been a standout feature. Apple has integrated cutting-edge technology like the H2 chip, allowing for richer, more balanced audio and dynamic adjustments to suit every user's hearing profile. This ensures that every listening experience, whether you're listening to your favorite music or catching up on a podcast, is optimized to suit your individual needs.

Hearing Health and Accessibility

The AirPods Pro 2's approach to hearing health is one of the most compelling aspects of this device. By becoming FDA-approved over-the-counter hearing aids, they've opened a new chapter in accessibility. They have effectively removed the barriers that have historically made hearing aids expensive and difficult to access, giving millions of people the ability to improve their hearing without the need for professional fitting or prescription.

Moreover, the inclusion of a self-assessment hearing test ensures that users can monitor their hearing health from the comfort of their homes. This level of convenience and accessibility represents Apple's commitment to inclusivity, allowing the AirPods Pro 2 to serve as both a consumer audio product and a crucial tool in hearing wellness. These advancements are a testament to Apple's understanding of the larger role their products play in everyday life—going beyond entertainment to also focus on health and well-being.

Integration with the Apple Ecosystem

One of the AirPods Pro 2's most impressive features is their seamless integration with the Apple ecosystem. Apple's ability to create a unified experience across its devices is unmatched in the tech industry, and the AirPods Pro 2 benefit greatly from this ecosystem. The ease of automatic pairing, device switching, and iCloud syncing make these earbuds the ideal accessory for users who own multiple Apple devices.

The AirPods Pro 2 enhance productivity by allowing users to transition from one device to another without the frustration of manually reconnecting their earbuds. Whether you're on a call on your iPhone, listening to music on your MacBook, or catching up on a show through your Apple TV, the AirPods Pro 2 make it effortless to stay connected to your devices.

Spatial audio and dynamic head tracking, which deliver an immersive, 3D sound experience, further enhance the AirPods Pro 2's role in the Apple ecosystem. These features elevate the AirPods Pro 2 beyond just earbuds for music and calls into an essential tool for watching movies, gaming, and other entertainment. They perfectly complement the Apple ecosystem's other products, adding a level of immersion and functionality that is difficult to replicate in competing devices.

User Experience and Real-World Impact

Throughout the chapters of this book, we've seen how the AirPods Pro 2 have made a tangible impact on real users. From people with hearing loss finding a discreet and effective solution to fitness enthusiasts using them to block out distractions during workouts, the AirPods Pro 2 have demonstrated their versatility. They are not just high-tech gadgets; they are everyday tools that improve people's lives.

Users have expressed how the AirPods Pro 2 have enhanced their productivity, daily routines, and even their social interactions. The ability to cancel out background noise during meetings or to switch seamlessly between devices makes them a must-have for professionals. On the other hand, the enhanced sound quality, long battery life, and comfort make them ideal for casual use—whether you're listening to music while working or enjoying a podcast on the go.

However, as with all products, the AirPods Pro 2 are not without their drawbacks. The limitations when used with non-Apple devices, for example, have been noted by several users. Automatic device switching and full integration with Apple's proprietary features are only available within the Apple ecosystem, which could be frustrating for users with a more diverse set of devices. Similarly, while the AirPods Pro 2 offer impressive battery life, there's always room for further improvement, particularly as users demand even longer usage times for all-day listening sessions.

The Role of AI and Machine Learning

As we look to the future of the AirPods Pro 2, artificial intelligence (AI) and machine learning will undoubtedly play a major role in shaping their capabilities. In future models, these technologies could make the AirPods Pro 2 even smarter by providing real-time audio adjustments, improving voice recognition for Siri, and offering even more personalized audio profiles.

Imagine a scenario where the AirPods Pro 2 use AI to automatically adjust the sound based on a user's environment, listening habits, and preferences. With machine learning, the earbuds could learn to fine-tune sound profiles based on daily usage patterns, adjusting automatically as you move between different environments. This level of personalization would make the AirPods Pro 2 even more intuitive and user-friendly, removing the need for manual adjustments altogether.

Furthermore, AI could enhance the health features of the AirPods Pro 2, providing deeper insights into users' hearing health and overall wellness. By continuously learning from users' feedback, the AirPods could even suggest lifestyle changes or recommend moments for rest based on the data gathered during listening sessions.

The Future of Audio and AirPods Pro in a Post-2025 World

As we enter the next decade, the role of AirPods Pro—and personal audio devices in general—will likely become even more integral to our daily lives. With the continued advancement of wireless technologies, spatial audio, and augmented reality, AirPods Pro could transform into something far beyond what we currently envision.

In a post-2025 world, the potential for the AirPods Pro to integrate seamlessly with augmented reality (AR) and virtual reality (VR) is immense. Apple has already made strides in AR with its ARKit framework, and future AirPods models could act as an essential part of this ecosystem. Imagine an experience where the AirPods Pro not only provide immersive 3D sound for movies and games but also serve as a conduit for interactive AR experiences, providing real-time sound cues, directional audio, and even haptic feedback as you navigate virtual environments.

Moreover, AirPods Pro could evolve into a full-fledged health and wellness device. With additional sensors and machine learning algorithms, future versions of the AirPods Pro could monitor a wide range of physical and mental health parameters, from stress levels to hydration to posture. In this vision of the future, the AirPods Pro would not only be a tool for entertainment and communication but also a comprehensive health assistant, offering users actionable insights into their well-being.

The Role of Sustainability

Sustainability will also be a crucial factor for Apple in the coming years. As consumers become more conscious of environmental issues, there is growing pressure on tech companies to reduce their carbon footprint. Future iterations of the AirPods Pro will likely see Apple continue to refine its sustainable practices, using more recycled materials and reducing electronic waste. Apple has already made strides in this area with the AirPods Pro 2, and it is likely that future models will focus even more on creating eco-friendly products that align with the company's broader commitment to carbon neutrality.

Conclusion: A Vision of Innovation, Accessibility, and Seamless Integration

In conclusion, the AirPods Pro 2 are more than just a piece of technology—they are a reflection of how far personal audio has come and a glimpse into the future of consumer electronics. With their combination of excellent sound quality, innovative features, and seamless integration into the Apple ecosystem, the AirPods Pro 2 have set a new standard for what truly wireless earbuds can achieve.

The future of the AirPods Pro is bright, filled with possibilities for smarter, more personalized listening experiences and deeper integration with health and wellness features. As AI and machine learning continue to shape the future of technology, the AirPods Pro will likely become even more intuitive, adaptive, and responsive to the needs of users.

In the next decade, we will see AirPods Pro evolve into a product that does more than just deliver great sound—it will serve as an essential tool for improving the quality of our lives. Whether it's enhancing our hearing health, helping us navigate augmented realities, or integrating more deeply into the smart homes of the future, the AirPods Pro 2 are a harbinger of the incredible potential for wireless audio technology in a rapidly changing world.

As Apple continues to innovate and refine its product offerings, it's clear that the AirPods Pro 2 will remain at the forefront of personal audio technology, blending seamless integration, cutting-edge features, and a user-centric approach to make them indispensable in the lives of millions around the world. The AirPods Pro 2 are not just a product; they are a part of a broader movement toward smarter, more connected living—an exciting glimpse into the future of personal technology.